# Financially Chic

Live a luxurious life on a budget, learn to love managing money, and grow your wealth

## FIONA FERRIS

ISBN-13: 978-1539076544
ISBN-10: 1539076547

This book is dedicated to... you.

May you enjoy being a shining example to those around you.

May you live richly and fully as you build your dream chic life

I know you can do it!

# CONTENTS

## Contents

FIONA FERRIS

# Introduction

I love to dream and plan how I can live a luxurious and beautiful life on a normal income and I also love to educate myself as much as I can about the world of money, so that I can feel empowered about my finances.

Back when I was younger and poorer, I fell into the credit card trap and was constantly paying off my Visa. It was no fun and I felt like I was on a treadmill because I was going to work each day to earn money which I had already spent. One day, I decided I had had enough, and did everything I could to get out of debt and focus on building wealth instead.

It was during this time that I became quite

skilled at living an 'expensive' life on a budget. I did not want to give up all my little luxuries, so I worked out ways to afford them or at least enjoyable alternatives to replace them with, so I could save money for the future. I do not mind telling you I became a real penny pincher and my family used to tease me about my frugal ways.

These days I have shifted my mindset to be one of abundance. However, my old background in thrift is still there and I believe having a combination of the two serves me very well. I am focused on financial expansion as well as being a thoughtful spender.

These days I get more of a thrill opening up a new investment account instead of going shopping. I do not want to waste money just for the sake of it and I am a firm believer that if you are a respectful steward of your money, your money will look after you.

Being this way is how my husband and I were able to pay off our first home within five years of buying it. It is so exciting to be mortgage-free and having the freedom to consider what we want to do next and I know I am not special. I know now that there is unlimited abundance and the same opportunities are available to everyone.

Instead of feeling constricted and broke when you are on a slim income or have debt to pay off, I invite you to look upon it as a fun and exciting adventure; where you can gain as much enjoyment as possible for the least amount of cost, as well as learning to get ahead financially. It feels creative and satisfying and will set you up for a lifetime of good habits, no matter the age you are starting from.

## How I became interested in personal finance

Money and financial management first caught my imagination in the early 1990s when I worked as a secretary for a financial planning firm. One of my jobs was to type up client reports and from that I could see the difference in wealth between people of the same age and in similar jobs.

I could also see there were people my age (early twenties at the time) who had already started investment portfolios, when I was more interested in shopping than investing. These were normal non-financial people like me, who were drip-feeding monthly amounts into investment plans to secure their future.

The amounts they were investing were not

large so they could still enjoy life now, but I knew from the graphs I had seen that a little bit each month added up to a sizeable amount in twenty, thirty or forty years' time.

Because I got to see so many different examples of wealth, my mind was opened to different ways of being, which I am very grateful for. This is when my journey into the world of money began, and because of this inspiring start, I still feel excited and it is like I have butterflies in my stomach when I hear a good savings or investment story – truly! I hope you feel the same way after reading *Financially Chic*.

## About this book

My wish for this book is that it encourages you to think about money in a way that makes you feel in control, uplifted and inspired to steer yourself towards a joyous and prosperous future.

I want to share my contagious beliefs that dealing with your money can be fun and exciting. I know many women have a fractious relationship with their finances and can often be quite scared of dealing with things. I have felt that way in the past too.

What I found out is that the bogey man is much scarier when you do not know him; once I started really looking into my money life, it seemed smaller and so much more manageable. The bogey man had shrunk to nothing because I had turned the light on.

I do hope you will join me in this journey because it feels so much better to have a good relationship with your money than not. I love the saying *Look after your money, and your money will look after you.*

It does not have to be scary, and you do not have to worry about becoming a greedy trollop if you focus on your finances; all that will happen is that this important area of your life will feel happier, freer and more bountiful. It is a glorious feeling and it is well within your reach.

I hope that by the end of this book you will be eager and enthusiastic about your own finances, in fact, I am sure you will.

# Chapter 1.

## *Start from the beginning*

I have often thought I would like to have been a financial counsellor; working one-on-one with people to increase their financial knowledge, showing them how simple tweaks and changes can change the course of their financial future dramatically and most importantly, *that it can be fun and enjoyable.*

I think that is how I have come to find myself in a good financial position – it was not one huge thing, but rather a lot of compounding small efforts that generated a snowball effect. At the same time, my quality of life remained good and I felt like I did not need to sacrifice that much. If you treat learning how to be savvy with money as a fun game, you will find it that much easier to meet your goals effortlessly.

I feel like I started out relatively late in life; I did not meet my husband until we were in our early thirties. We both had a small amount of money (*quite* small), but no assets such as property and, thankfully, no debt. I owned a car (my husband had a company car) and we each had a few pieces of furniture.

Within a few years, however we were running a successful small business together. Several years after that we had paid off our business loan and bought our first home with a 30% deposit which we had saved, and now, thirteen years after we first met, our home is paid off in full and we are contemplating a major lifestyle change.

We are excited to be in the process of selling our business, then our home, and moving to the small town where I grew up. We want to live a slow and peaceful life and we are making it happen now, in our mid-forties, instead of waiting for retirement.

We still plan on working, of course. However, because we have a financial cushion, it is not so imperative that we get a job the very next week. Anytime I have moved cities in the past, I have finished one job on the Friday, moved over the weekend and started my new job on the Monday because I had to, like many people do.

When my husband and I first met, we thought we would always be on the back foot money-wise simply because we got together at a later age. Others around us had met and married in their twenties (or even high school) and had been homeowners for years. Then we both left our jobs to start our own small business and our wages dropped dramatically *and* we were still renting.

We loved being self-employed and were happy to be running our own business, but this move meant we were even further behind our friends and people around us.

We got married during those lean years and had a measly two days off work for our wedding, simply because that was as long as we could get someone to look after our business for us. We did not have our honeymoon until six years after our marriage (eight nights in Hawaii – it was wonderful).

We would save money every way we knew how. We religiously scanned the supermarket brochures each week for specials and had a pricing notebook that we would write our grocery prices in so we would know when a special was good.

Looking back at those days that were not so long ago, it is hard to believe we are now embarking on a new life that has been made possible by our good financial fortune. Is it luck though or is it something else?

I believe it is a combination of many factors, including the choices we made day-to-day; the vision we had for the life we wished to lead; the fact that we were both reading from the same page; and also of having a long-term view. I look forward to going through all my success secrets with you in the following chapters.

First though, I would like to make the disclaimer that I am *not* a financial planner. However, I have a passion for the subject of money management. I have read a ton of books over the past twenty-five years; budgeted and run the accounts for myself and now our household and business, and never lost the faith that whilst I am building up towards greatness in the future, I still want to have a fabulous time today. And you can too.

## What do you believe about money?

Growing up, most of us were only exposed to our immediate family in terms of money and knowing what we can expect from life; and even then, our parents do not usually discuss the big financial picture with their children. For the most part, we earned pocket money and had part-time jobs and also absorbed our family's messages about how good or bad money was.

In addition, it often seemed that money caused stress. There was not enough or sometimes there were financial crises. I am not just talking about my own family, but what I saw on television programmes and in movies too. Often these messages taught us to be scared of money and fearful of our future.

From what I saw in popular media, none of us really had any control over our financial future and it was something to be constantly concerned about. At that time, I almost believed that it was mere luck if I ended up comfortable in retirement.

See if you have heard of any of these common sayings:

*Money does not grow on trees*

*We are not made of money*

*Rich people are greedy*

*Rich people exploit others*

*You have to rip others off in order to make money*

*I do not need to be rich, I just want to be happy*

*It is wrong to want more than you have*

*Just be happy with what you've got*

*You will have to save hard and sacrifice now, so you won't be poor in retirement*

Can you relate to any of these money beliefs? How do you think they may have impacted the way you've interacted with money without even realising it?

From all the reading, research and study I have done over the years, I now know that none of these things need to be true; they are simply beliefs we have taken on from others and made our own. Certainly there are examples of evil or greedy rich people, but equally there are examples of evil people with no money (and rich people who do good with their wealth).

It may be that we are subconsciously washing our hands of being good with money because, for example, we have an underlying belief that wealthy people are greedy and exploitative and we do not want to be like that.

However, money does not have the power to change us. *Money simply makes us more of who we already are.* If we think we might become greedy and exploitative if we had more money, we would have to be greedy and exploitative before being wealthier.

If we are kind-hearted and caring now; once we have more money we will simply be a richer person who is kind-hearted and caring, so we will likely support charities close to our heart or help others in some way. We will also go about earning money in a kind-hearted and caring way.

At its most basic, money is simply a symbol of an exchange in energy between two people. It is a way that was developed thousands of years ago because it was easier to work with than the bartering system, which was the way of exchange at the time.

Swapping two goats for some building work

was a problematic equation if you were the builder and did not need or want two goats. Coins were made from gold and silver and these were traded instead.

Over time the system has been refined, and nowadays physical money is not even required since we have digital methods of transferring funds to the person or company we are doing business with.

Some budgeting systems advocate going back to the notes and coins method if you want to get a handle on your money situation, because it seems more real than swiping a plastic card or clicking a 'buy now' button.

It certainly is very easy to pay with our credit or debit card and forget we are actually spending money.

## Make your finances fun and enjoyable

Before I learned how to enjoy managing my finances, the main messages I used to sense around personal finance were:

*It is uncontrollable. I have no control over my financial future – luck and circumstance decides.*

*It is boring, dry and dull to sort the money stuff, so avoid looking at it unless I absolutely have to.*

*Wealth is for other people, not me. I will live a normal life where I pay off a mortgage until I retire, then live off a modest living from my retirement savings.*

*If I am lucky, I will marry someone rich and I won't have to worry about money.*

I do not know about you, but these beliefs did not inspire me to want anything to do with my bank account, except to have fun spending what I had earned. Whenever I started an ambitious savings plan, I would become discouraged six months down the track when I saw how the money had not grown much at all. *There's no use, I might as well enjoy it now,* I would think.

It was not until I started my financial planning secretarial role that my eyes were opened to a new way of being. Add to this, one of my bosses who studied personal development (which I had never heard of), loaned me his cassette tapes – yes, it was a long time ago! – of motivational speaker Brian Tracy and all of a sudden a fire was lit underneath me.

There was a new and exciting way to be, and it all started in my head. I listened to those tapes over and over and faithfully did the exercises. Even though this was thrilling to me, not much changed.

Maybe I needed time for all the information to sink in and percolate around, I do not know, but I do know that nothing done is ever wasted. I am so grateful to that early inspiration twenty-five years ago because it started me on a path to wealth which came about in a fun, inspiring and simple way.

What I did not realise at the time when I was looking for instant results, is that it was all the little steps I was taking each day; all those decisions towards my financial goals that added up over time.

Yes, people can take quantum leaps, but more often the overnight success stories have been reading, inspiring and working on themselves behind the scenes long before they popped up glossy and shiny. And you can be a success story for yourself if you want.

It does not matter what age you are: please hear me when I tell you it is never too late to take more of an interest in your finances. Of course in an ideal world we would all have our interest piqued as a ten-year old and be well on our way in our twenties and thirties, however if you are not this age, it does not matter.

You can feel happier about your current circumstances and improve on them from today, gaining enormous benefits no matter how old you are now.

## Simplify your life

My first step to a better financial future was to step back and take stock of how I filled my life. I had been going through my months and years on auto-pilot and I will never forget the shocking realization I got one day as I did yet another declutter of my closet.

I had always prided myself on being an excellent declutterer because I was forever donating boxes and bags of clothing to the charity shops. If that was the case, the one thing I could not understand was why my wardrobe always felt full; but, you guessed it, I would go shopping every weekend and on most lunch breaks for entertainment. I did not always buy things, but as you know, the more you browse, the more temptation there is.

My wardrobe was like a revolving door and I wondered why I never seemed to be able to save money. When I made the connection with my constant shopping to my empty bank account, I stopped shopping almost overnight. It is a fairly obvious connection I am sure you will agree, but when you are enjoying all your lovely new goodies, it is an easy one to ignore.

Funnily enough, this cured my full-to-the-brim wardrobe 'problem'. From then on, I wore and enjoyed the clothing I had, eventually replacing an item here or there as I needed to (it took me a while to get to that point).

Instead of feeling poorer because I could no longer shop, I actually felt empowered that I was not giving other people all my money. I loved the feeling of my savings banking up, and I loved using and caring for what I had. It made me appreciate everything so much more.

With my personal development work, I realised that I would shop to feel good, and that this somehow related to self-worth. In addition, I also saw that I ate for the same reason sometimes – to fill that hollow emptiness inside.

Once I stopped shopping and focused on other things in my life – more satisfying pursuits – my self-worth increased. It is an upward spiral because the better you feel about yourself, the less you self-sabotage with your actions.

I went back to the hobbies and interests I

enjoyed as a school girl and found a more grounding way to live. I started to knit again, did a few sewing projects, read more books and started writing my own inspirational stories and articles. I was also walking daily after work and loved that connection to nature after a day in the office.

I felt I was on a good track again, where shopping receded into the background, and was not up front as a main part of my emotional life as it had been.

Perhaps you can relate to this? Consider that there might be areas in your life that you are filling up on unnecessarily and with the wrong things, because you are feeling 'less than' in yourself. In what ways do you get out of control sometimes, and if you were a person looking in, what would you say they were linked to? Perhaps there are some changes you can make to redirect your focus?

# Chapter 2.

## *Be savvy and a good steward of your money*

There are only two ways to become better off financially – make more money or cut back. It is simply the law of common sense that if you spend more than you earn, there will be tears at some stage. So, you can either spend less than you earn, or earn more than you spend.

In the beginning, my only technique was to cut back, and that certainly moved us forward very quickly. However, as I read more about the flow of abundance and the law of attraction, I realised I was only focusing on one side of the coin, so to speak. There was another whole side and it was the positive side (abundance).

Focusing only on cutting back can bring about a feeling of lack or poverty consciousness, if it is the only thing you have in your mind like I used to.

Cutting back definitely helps turn the ship around very quickly, especially if you do a complete audit of all your expenses. I have found that setting a big money goal whether it is saving a certain amount or paying off a debt by a certain time, helps flush out those expenses that you do not really care that much about.

It might be a recurring subscription that you could take or leave, going shopping for leisure or weekly meals out. In these cases, you could decide to delete the subscription, go walking in the park for leisure and meeting your friends for coffee instead of brunch, for example.

Now I do both – make more money *and* cut back – and think it is a more balanced way to be.

I am not only about penny-pinching and scrimping to be better off financially any more. I would rather focus on abundance and wealth and being fruitful because it feels much better to me. And because what you focus on grows, why not focus on increasing your financial abundance rather than cutting corners and feeling pinched.

In saying that, I totally support saving money where possible, when you can do it in a way that feels good. I love to find swaps where I can save money without sacrificing quality. Sometimes the cheaper version is actually an upgrade, which is a nice surprise.

One aspect of cutting costs that many people do not realise, and I certainly did not until my husband pointed it out, is that there is a tax benefit. Yes, a tax benefit. Now, do not leave me hanging on the page here and disappear out of the room because 'tax' is such a boring and/or scary word. There are no financial tax returns involved, I promise.

The simple premise is this – money saved is 'tax-free' money. You have not had to earn it so you are not taxed on it. Let me illustrate for you: To spend $100, you have to earn that amount. However, you will be taxed on it – say you are on a 30% tax rate. You then have only $70 to spend once you have paid your tax. But if you choose *not* to spend $100 and look for an alternative option, that is a whole $100 tax-free 'earned' right there.

You will be saving even more if you put the money saved onto your mortgage or credit card debt because of the interest you won't need to pay on that $100.

There are a multitude of ways to save money without feeling like you are cutting back; usually it is by changing things you do habitually, and I will share with you my favourites in this chapter.

## Living well on a moderate income

When my husband and I were saving for our first home deposit on extremely modest incomes, we really did watch every penny. We are a little more relaxed now; however, many of the habits we adopted to save money then, we still do today.

And equally, sometimes it is habits that can sink you because you do them without thinking any more. Take a look at your spending habits and see if there are any ways you are 'leaking' money that does not bring you any benefit.

Brian Tracy talks about zero-based thinking, which means you are taking decision making right back to the start. Say you have five magazine subscriptions that just keep coming in month after month, and they are on an auto-renewal service. You look forward to some, merely flick through others and do not really think about it month-to-month.

If you asked yourself *Do I enjoy all of these*

*subscriptions and gain immense value and enjoyment from every one of them?* and the answer is not a resounding *YES* for each one, consider cancelling the subscription. That is free money you have just found.

Here are some of the ways we have cut costs painlessly:

**Cook more meals at home** each week. Not only do you have a superior meal for lesser cost, but you can make it really enjoyable, as well as improving your cooking skills. Set the table with candles and make it special, or feel naughty by eating on the sofa with a movie. There are no other diners to annoy you, you do not have to pay extra if you want a coffee after dinner and there is no travel time.

Make your main meal the focus of your day rather than a chore to be avoided. Plan ahead what ingredients you need, shop for them and prepare them. Enjoy this process instead of enduring it.

**Create new rituals**. We used to often go out for brunch at a café on a Sunday morning. One day we decided to recreate that at home; partly this was inspired by a romantic notion in my head of how a couple in the movies lounge around in pajamas in the morning with weekend brunch and the newspapers.

We made our favourite café food and coffee – it was not hard – and bought the Sunday papers. This became our favourite new thing to do. The bonus is that when we did go out for brunch, it was more special because we did not do it every week.

**Consider sharing a car** if possible. Because we run our business together, my husband and I choose to share a car (he had to give his company car back when he left his job). Almost thirteen years later, we are still happily sharing a car. Every so often we will think *Oh, it would be nice to have two cars*, but one of us will talk the other out of it and we stick with one. It really is not much more of a hassle and we can take the bus if we need to (we live in a big city though; once we live in a small town, taking public transport may not be such a viable option).

I am sure we will buy a second car someday, but in the meantime we have saved a lot on not only the purchase price, but insurance, registration, servicing and fuel. There would probably be more trips if the second car was there, whereas at the moment we plan our errands for certain days. The longer we can do this the more we are saving, and when we do have two cars at some stage, it will seem like Christmas every day!

For instance, if I am having a day off at home while my husband is at our business, I do not often go out because there is no car available to me. I might walk to nearby shops if I need something, but mostly I plan ahead, and I love being at home so it is not a hardship to me. Occasionally I have caught the bus to an appointment. If I had a car available to me, I am sure I would have 'popped out' more often, and unnecessarily as well.

You might not choose to sell your second car, but when it comes to the stage where you need to replace a vehicle, perhaps consider a trial of 3-6 months where you share a car. It actually feels quite freeing; you will save money, plus I find I feel more European when I make trips or go shopping with intention and on foot.

**Try the budget options**. When I have tried the budget option of something I have been doing, sometimes it has worked out, and sometimes it has not.

I might have tried a budget grocery option and it was terrible (such as the liquid laundry detergent with the consistency of water) so I went back to my first choice, or I might have tried it and was thrilled (my new low-price hairdresser).

You will never know until you try, so why not re-evaluate your choices every once in a while.

**Stay at home more**. On my days off work, I used to love browsing the shops because I thought staying at home and doing the housework was so boring. Not only was I spending money unnecessarily, but my house was still in the same dusty and untidy state that I had left it. My new purchases did not look so appealing once I arrived back home.

Since I made the change to mostly staying at home, and shopping/browsing less regularly, my home looks better because I have decluttered it (making it much more appealing to stay in), plus it is more satisfying. Shopping for stuff you do not need brings such an empty feeling and it does not feel good.

**Make an evening out of one thing**. I have never understood the dinner and a movie concept. Whenever we have done it with friends, we are always rushing through our food, keeping an eye on the clock and then bolting out to catch our movie. It is less enjoyable, *and* you are paying more. Lose/lose!

I prefer instead to do one thing per night, either dinner, a movie or concert if we are going out. You then get to enjoy that experience with no hurry, and you are spreading out your spending.

**Visit/invite a friend to your home** instead of meeting out. I have lady friends whom I get together with every so often for lunch or a coffee. Sometimes it is nice to entertain them at home instead, or in the case of an elderly friend, I offer to take lunch with me to her place. It is less expensive overall and I find it more relaxing too.

**Recreate takeout meals at home.** One of my favourite hobbies (if you could call it that) is to recreate our favourite takeout meals at home. Sometimes I buy ready-made components of a meal, however it still works out healthier and less expensive to do this.

So far we have tried homemade fish and chips, Indian curry and rice, pizzas, souvlaki, nachos and even our own 'Chili's dinner' which is homemade seasoned crumbed chicken tenders and dipping sauces with coleslaw, and either baked potato and sour cream or homemade sweet potato wedges and aioli.

We saw Chili's in Hawaii on our honeymoon and actually did not end up eating there, but looking at the menu gave us ideas for our casual Sunday night dinners. I think it is quite funny that we have our version of a Chili's dinner never having been a customer.

Of course 'takeout' meals are not regular occurrences because they are not as healthy and vege-rich as our normal meals, but they are a nice option from time to time.

**Growing your own vegetables** or at least fresh herbs. A vegetable garden gives you something to do in the weekend so you are not out spending money. It is satisfying to have done some planting and even weeding (so much more than shopping or entertainment) plus you save money when you get to eat your harvest.

Herbs particularly are expensive to buy, but easy and inexpensive to grow. In addition, you often only need a small amount for a recipe, and it is easy to pop outside and pick them. You do not need a lot of room, just a few pots if you do not have a garden.

An added bonus is that when you grow your own herbs and vegetables, you know they have not had commercial pesticides sprayed all over them, which is possibly the best reason of all to grow your own.

**Look at your utility bills**. Can you switch companies for a better deal whether it comes to cell phones, Internet, electricity or gas? It can be an arduous task, but comparing plans can bring big savings, and as these bills are every month, the savings mount up.

When I was visiting my mum recently, she complained how high her phone bill was. I looked at her latest bill and went through all the items line by line. I asked her if she used a particular service I could see was listed. She did not know she even had that service on her account, so I offered to ring and question it. She didn't want the bother and said not to call them.

Well, I did ring and she was not happy as I hung around on hold for ages. This was not a fun way for her to spend time with her daughter! After half an hour I had spoken with someone who told me that my mum had had this service for almost a year, *and no-one had told her when it was added*. They agreed to refund a back-dated amount as they could see she had never used it, and it was removed from her account going forward.

The result of this is that she received a free month of service thanks to the refund, and her ongoing bill is much lower. No, it's not a fun way to spend time, but sometimes you have to do it and the results are worth it.

When I had a non-smartphone, I paid only $9 a month for talk and text; it was the cheapest plan I could find. Then, when I bought a smartphone, my plan went up to $19 a month, which was still far cheaper than anything else I had seen around.

Most of the time I have my data switched off. When I am at home my phone uses our Wi-Fi, and when I am out I usually only switch my data on to send an email or check something else. Sometimes if I am out for the day I will leave the data on as a treat. I know, I am pretty frugal if I consider this a treat.

**Revisit your mortgage**. When we bought our first home, we split the amount on fixed and floating interest rates. The floating rate meant we could pay off extra amounts without penalty. The fixed rate was a slightly lower interest rate, but there was a limit to how much extra you could pay toward your debt.

We thought we were quite clever splitting the mortgage, until our accountant upped the game by advising us to change our floating portion to a revolving credit account because of our business. Our business earnt money each day, but we only needed it once a month to pay the bills. In the meantime, we transferred those funds daily to our revolving credit account which saved us a huge amount of interest on our mortgage.

This method may work for you, even if you do not have a business. If you use your credit card for everyday expenses and pay the balance off in full each month, getting up to 55-days interest-free credit means that same money could sit in your revolving credit account, off-setting your mortgage interest while you wait for the due date of your credit card payment.

The only (and very important) warning I would make to you, is that if you find it hard to restrain yourself from spending money, do **not** take the revolving credit option up. Worst case scenario is that you could spend your house, because all the equity in your home is available to you, instantly.

Naturally, with any changes you consider making to your mortgage, talk to your accountant or a bank advisor first.

## Add up what your vice is costing you

David Bach, in his excellent book '*The Automatic Millionaire*', talks about The Latte Factor. David reminded his readers that small amounts often, add up to a lot over time. He was criticized for this by many coffee fans who said they enjoyed their morning brew every day. I recently heard an interview with David where he said he was misunderstood. Coffee was only illustrating the point; he said there were many other ways in which we fritter away large amounts over the years via our daily habits.

For me, I used to have breakfast at home before work, but I would buy coffee and a muffin on the way to work, and then buy sushi for lunch, both five days a week. I would estimate I was spending $65 per week on lunch and a snack, which works out to $4,000 per year or $17,000 for the five years I worked at that job in the city.

If I had done then what I do now, which is make my own lunch and coffee most days, I could have bought a car with the difference! Yes, I still needed to buy grocery items to make my lunch and coffee at home, but there would still have been a sizeable amount left over.

These days I enjoy making coffee each day

at home. I brew up my Bialetti espresso-maker with find-grind coffee and pour a small amount into my cup, topping up with soy milk and heating in the microwave. I really enjoy this and, equally enjoy having a bought coffee every once in a while. It is definitely more of a treat to me now than when I bought one most days.

Think about *your* habits. What same things do you spend money on day in and day out?

Where I work at the moment, a slim and elegant lady from the business next door walks past us every morning with a Diet Coke from the convenience store. If she wants a Coke every day, surely it would be an easy decision to buy a multi-pack from the supermarket and put one in the fridge each night or bring it to work with her in the morning?

Little things like that, that are so easy to do boggle my mind. I think most people think to themselves *Oh, it is not that much, it is only a few dollars*, but when you add it up over time, it is worth changing that habit.

## Try out cheaper options

When I was in my twenties, I used high-end cosmetics, skincare and perfume exclusively. I was very snobby about low-cost products and would not be caught dead shopping at the grocery store in the cosmetic aisle.

Then, I landed my dream job, well, the job itself was not a dream, it was office administration, but the company was Christian Dior cosmetics. I was in heaven! We were able to purchase at staff rates and there was even a staff allocation of one product free of charge each month. We could also buy 'dented boxes' at a steeply reduced rate.

When I left five years later to join the business my husband started, I found it difficult to pay full retail for products I had previously enjoyed using at discounted rates. Add to this our reduced wages as we got our business going, and it was then that I started trying supermarket skincare brands.

Happily, they seemed to be lovely products and I wondered *Have I been wasting my money all these years?* I still do not know the answer to that, but what I do know is that I am still using and loving inexpensive skincare and cosmetics. My one product that I would always buy expensive was foundation, but even those have improved immensely.

If you do have a favourite prestige product that you have to have, look out for special offers such as a gift with purchase or free facial event when you do want to replace something.

## 'The free part'

Aside from being frugal, I am also respectful of resources. What I mean by this, is that I feel disrespectful if I throw away an item that is still useful. If it can be fixed well and easily, I will fix it. If I do not like something anymore, I will donate it. It upsets me when I see good items thrown into skips on home renovation or decluttering shows (and the item is often broken as a result of being thrown in, so I know they are not going to take it somewhere else to donate afterwards).

One day I told my dad I had glued my hairbrush handle back together again and he said *That's the free part*, which I thought was such a great saying. I think of it often now, and when I cut open a lotion tube to use up the last bit (there is always a lot left in there), I say to myself *That's the free part*, because a lot of people would never use it up.

I am not saying to use an item that is broken beyond repair, or so dirty that it cannot be cleaned anymore, because that is a fast way to feeling depressed and like you are living in a pit. Rather, by using 'the free part' in a way that feels good to me, I feel like I am not wasting resources since I am using an item up (whether it is a consumable or not).

It will be different for each of us what we feel is acceptable. For me, if a glass or cup has a chip, I throw it out immediately, whereas that might not bother someone else. Overall though, I would say I keep things longer than most people; by using, washing, fixing and mending. Generally, any clothing donated now is because I have chosen a style or colour that does not suit me; and, because I am much choosier about what I buy, those items are virtually non-existent.

If it is appropriate, more often I will downgrade public clothing to home clothing. Please note if something is damaged or stained, it is thrown out; I would not wear anything at home that I could not be seen in public in; it is just that sometimes you notice clothing is not quite as pristine as it once was, and you no longer feel good about wearing it when you go out.

Naturally you would not repurpose a blazer and pencil skirt to wear at home, but I am lucky enough that my workplace is quite casual so I can easily downgrade work clothing to home clothing. I also like to make sure the majority of my clothing is machine-washable. I do not like the chemicals, cost or inconvenience of dry-cleaning, and I am not a great hand washer (you know how those items sit in the bottom of your laundry hamper wash after wash?)

## Cap limits in your life

I love this method of keeping life simple. Some choose to have, for example, thirty hangers in their wardrobe, and when they run out of hangers they have to swap out and declutter an item, if they want to introduce something new to their wardrobe.

For me, excess books have been an issue in the past; what can I say, I just love books. However, some were novels I was not planning on reading again, others were on subjects I was no longer interested in; and yet more were books that although I always planned on reading them, I just never got around to it. Sometimes the font was tiny or the pages unappealing; it does not take much for me to pass over a book.

I have a bookshelf unit which is divided into a dozen cubes. I also have a ladder-style single-width bookshelf, that my talented dad made me from a picture I showed him. I have had a few big book declutters, and my rule is that all my books have to fit on those two shelving units. It works too, because if I buy a few books and find I am horizontally stacking them on top of the books I already have, I know it is time for another declutter.

As with my constant clothing declutter, knowing I would have to get rid of some books before I bought any more has made me a friend of the public library. Nowadays, books have to reach strict criteria to deserve a place in my home library. They are often books I have already borrowed from the public library to see if I would read them again beyond the one-month library loan period.

The exception is when I browse second-hand books in charity shops. I love to keep an eye out for older or out-of-print books. Or sometimes if a novel looks good and it is only $1 to buy, read and re-donate, I will do that. I have supported the charity with the purchase price, I do not have to read it by a certain library due date, plus the charity gets to sell it again when I have finished. It is definitely a win/win, but even then I have to be careful, because it could end up being one more book on my to-read pile.

Our pantry is quite small overall which caps our plates and glasses nicely; our weekly groceries are well thought out too, because there is only a limited amount of room for everything to be stored.

Is there anything more stressful than an overstuffed pantry? When ours gets too full, I do not like the suffocating feeling it gives me when I am trying to locate an ingredient, plus items get forgotten about and can pass their expiry date. What a waste!

When our pantry does get a bit close to the brim, I take *all* the food items out and put them on the kitchen counter. After a quick wipe of the shelves, I then put everything back neatly, checking items for age as I go. Sometimes I will find items I had forgotten buying, so I make a plan to use them up soon. Often the pantry is just messy because items get put back haphazardly; organizing the items helps restore order and serenity.

Capping limits helps enormously with your finances too, because you are naturally limiting spending. It feels better because you are not saying to yourself 'you can't buy that', instead you are choosing to keep your possessions within pre-chosen limits; limits that you know will enhance your life.

## Decide for yourself what you splurge and save on

It is quite fascinating just how different we all are. What I might naturally spend frugally on, someone else would never consider it and go for the expensive option without thinking. And vice versa – what *you* choose without thought might be wildly extravagant to another.

My late maternal nana bought herself beautiful, expensive shoes, yet would balk at the price of a long-distance phone call. She would keep flat soft drink in her fridge (it did not matter that it was not fizzy any more, there was still liquid in the bottle to use up) yet happily spend quite a bit on a bottle of brandy.

We all have our items that we are happy to splurge and save on and this is just one way we can cut back without too much sacrifice, by choosing the areas we are happy to save on. It will be different for everyone.

For me, I am happy to buy home-brand grocery items most of the time, but I love my avocados which can be quite expensive at certain times of the year. I buy most fruit and vegetables in season, however prices can still vary a lot. I used not to buy them when I considered them 'too dear', but I gave myself a wake-up call when I realised I would happily pay $3 for junky chocolate, but not an avocado or some strawberries, or even a bunch of spring flowers. My priorities were clearly a little skewed and I am glad I saw this.

## Spend more time at home

Making home such a welcoming place to be that you would rather spend time there than anywhere else, is a fantastic way to save money whilst still having a high quality of life. Being an introvert, home is my favourite place to be anyway, and if you are an extrovert it may be more challenging.

However, there are many things we might automatically do outside of the home that we can exchange for at-home options, such as:

Dining
Exercising
Socialising
Watching a movie

The bonus is, when you spend more time at home you are making the most of our home too. An example could be choosing to spend time in the garden instead of browsing the mall, or redecorating your bedroom instead of going away for the weekend.

I am not saying be a hermit and never go out, but choosing to switch something once a week or a couple of times a month will add up. *Every little bit* adds up. My father-in-law says that as soon as you pass the letterbox you put your hand in your pocket, and it is so true! Even if it is just parking or a coffee, you will be lucky to get away without spending anything once you go out.

For our last birthday (my husband and I were born on the same day, one year apart), we decided that instead of going out for dinner, we would have a nice dinner at home that neither of us would have to cook. How did we do that? By purchasing snacky yummy treats and having a rolling feast while we watched a Woody Allen movie. It was a wonderful evening.

We had cheese, crackers and bread, sushi rolls, a few hot items heated in the oven (*hors d'oeuvre* types), small bowls of olives and nuts, and gourmet ice-cream and French macarons afterwards. It was such an enjoyable evening and we did not even care that we had saved money; we would likely choose it again even if it cost the same as dinner out, because we both had such a great time.

## Make your own meals most of the time

This is simultaneously the easiest and the hardest change to make. When you are not in the groove of cooking at home, it can seem a monumental task and expensive to set your kitchen up with grocery staples, fresh fruit, vegetables and condiments. In which case you might think *Blow it, let's eat out tonight.*

There seems to be a lot more pre-prepared food available from supermarkets these days, so maybe this is a good in-between place to start. When you are a true cook-at-home person, those ready-packs seem quite expensive; but when you are used to restaurant or take-out prices they will seem like a bargain. You will then get your confidence up to cook at home more.

Start with your favourite meals to order when you are out, and buy the ingredients for those. You will need fresh ingredients and herbs, spices and other pantry staples such as breadcrumbs or pasta etc. These can be used for the next meal of this type as well. Then add another meal, and another to your repertoire.

We mostly eat healthy meals – 5-6 nights a week – however on Sundays we might make something like nachos or a 'pub dinner' such as crumbed chicken tenders, baked potato or chips and coleslaw. That is actually my favourite project – make a homemade (and healthier) version of your favourite restaurant or takeout meal.

My husband is a big fan of hamburgers, whereas I am not. There is a lot of bread which I find very filling, plus they are just so messy to eat. Having stuff on my hands and squidging between my fingers grosses me out!

I had an idea that would make us both happy though – I bought some greaseproof paper and made homemade cheeseburgers and oven fries (plus coleslaw). I bought smaller buns for myself and I had a 'single patty/one slice of cheese' burger, and my husband had a normal sized bun with two patties and two slices of cheese. For the oven fries, I sliced scrubbed floury potatoes and sprayed with olive oil. They are quick to make and far nicer than frozen fries (and a much lower cost as well, I am sure).

My *pièce de résistance* was to wrap our burgers in greaseproof paper once I had built them. This served two purposes, three actually. Firstly, it kept them warm, secondly they were much tidier to eat from the wrap and my hands stayed clean, and thirdly, my husband was so impressed with the 'realistic' wrapped burger and chips on his plate.

It was such a fun meal to make and eat, and okay, it was not the lightest meal I have ever had, but it was still a lot healthier than a bought hamburger meal and a lot less in cost for the high quality of the ingredients.

This meal was simple and easy to make, scored massive husband brownie points and is just one of my examples that you do not have to suffer to save money.

## Do not be afraid to ask for gifts

I am not a big fan of gift giving and in fact I am trying to persuade my family that there is no need to exchange birthday and Christmas gifts – I would rather receive good wishes instead of pressuring people with obligation purchasing. But until that time comes, I happily offer gift suggestions when I am asked. My mum in particular always asks if there is anything I would like for my birthday or Christmas, or else she threatens me with something horrible – 'knick knacks and cloggers' as my brother calls unwanted home items.

If there is something I have my eye on, I tell her. For my fortieth birthday I asked for a high-quality hairdryer, and I am still happily using it several years later. It is a great outcome all round – my mum has not wasted her money on something I might not like and therefore will declutter, and I am the very happy recipient of a higher quality item than I might have purchased for myself.

If you exchange gifts with family members or friends, why not ask them if there is a book they would like, or a magazine they would love a subscription to (if you cannot persuade them to agree not to swap gifts, of course). It feels so good to give a gift that is truly wanted and loved, plus you are saved the stress of coming up with a good present. An excellent outcome all round!

## Slim down your magazine choices

I am such a sucker for magazines that I shudder to think how much I have spent on them over the years, considering they are a disposable product which are donated or recycled after you have read them. If I added up all the money from my years of magazine buying, I probably could have invested in a rental property instead. Still, until they invent time travel, all I can do is start from today.

Look at the titles you purchase/subscribe to on a regular basis and ask yourself if you love them all and get good value for the amount they cost you. You may wish to borrow them instead. If you do not belong to your local public library, I highly encourage you to join up. Libraries have changed a lot and these days offer not just books, but magazines, DVDs and CDs too.

I decided on my favourite title – *Victoria* – and subscribed (which is half the price of buying it in a store) and I happily order others I like from our library – *Vogue, Hello, Martha Stewart Living*. I even started ordering car, men's fashion and movie magazines from the library for my husband and he loves reading them. I am so grateful for our public library service and happily pay our property taxes because of this service alone.

Another way I feel like I am living a rich life on a budget, is when I request all the latest books I have read great reviews of. Sometimes they can take a while to come in but I do not mind, I have got plenty in my library queue so I am *never* short of something to read, and it is always exciting to receive a 'new' book.

If it is a novel, I am happy to read and return it; if it is a non-fiction book, I am grateful for the chance to borrow it for a month and decide if it is a candidate for my home library. Sometimes I borrow books more than once to decide if I

really want them. This cuts down on clutter as
well as unnecessary expense.

# Chapter 3.

## *Live like a millionaire now and feel rich every day*

Now we get to the fun part, not that saving money isn't fun, but dreaming up ways to live an expensive life without spending a lot of money is *more fun*. I love finding new ways to feel rich, whilst still living my everyday life.

The key for me to feel good about diverting much of our meagre income into savings and then a mortgage was to *cultivate the feeling of richness every day*. There are so many ways to feel rich and I am going to share some of my favourites with you in this chapter.

The other important thing is to feel happy and excited for the good things you are building towards – you are creating wealth for yourself and your family by thinking this way and making sacrifices. The fantastic thing is that when you have fun along the way, they do not feel like sacrifices.

Doing all the things that make you feel good is so important, because they anchor in the feeling you are wanting to create when you have more money. By experiencing them now, not only are you enjoying your life more as you get there, but you are 'acclimatizing' yourself to uplevel over time.

## Do not wait to be rich to feel good

Many of us, including me in the past, think *One day when I am richer, everything will be perfect. I won't have any problems because I will have enough money to do everything I want to.*

As I *did* become richer, because every time you receive a pay increase or finish paying off a debt, you *are* richer; the money seemed to be absorbed into something else and I felt the same.

It is not that there was the same amount of

money, it is just that you get used to things being a certain way, so it is unlikely that one day you will wake up feeling amazing and saying *I am rich today!* because you have suddenly received a million dollars in the bank. Unless you buy lottery tickets that is unlikely to happen, and even if you do, it is still unlikely (just saying).

Really, we could all wake up each morning and shout *I am rich today!* because we actually are, but that is a topic for another chapter. However, it does prove to us that we can make the decision to be rich, and behave from a place as if we already have the things we desire around us.

Then, when we do gain our heart's desires, we will be ready for them.

One example could be your car. Imagine driving your old bomb around and fantasizing about the day when you can buy a brand new European car. You are saving and getting closer and you know it will not be long.

However, in the meantime you do not treat your old car well. You think it is not worth it to have an annual service, you do not wash it and the interior is full of bits and bobs. You know that when you have your dream car one day though, that you will treat that car well.

Can you see where I am going here? When

you eventually buy your brand new European car, you are not in the habit of looking after it. You forget about the groceries on the back seat one night and the next day you drive to work with them still there. A tomato rolls out of the bag and under the seat, so that you do not notice it when you take the groceries in that night.

There is a strange smell as the tomato rots into the carpet under your seat but you cannot see anything obvious, so you do not worry about it and eventually the smell goes away.

You do not clean or dust the interior, the windows are dirty and the paint job only sees a wash when it rains. Before too long, you are feeling just like you did with your old car.

Imagine instead, if you treated your old bomb just like it was your dream car. You emptied it of shopping, gym bags and trash every night. You cleaned it regularly and kept it serviced and maintained.

You will then have good habits when it comes to your new car. The end result is that you feel great about your old car *and* you are equally as excited to be looking forward to your new car one day.

## Use your good things

Why would you not want to use all your best possessions now? It is so easy to want to save things up but really, why not live today as if it is your last, enjoying everything wonderful that you already own? You know you could be hit by a bus tomorrow, right?

Instead of keeping the good sheets for 'one day' or guests, use them now. That expensive scented candle your husband gave you for your birthday? Light it today. Those premium samples you were given at the cosmetic counter? Do not save them for your next trip, use them tonight and *enjoy them*. There are likely as many examples like these around your home as there are at my place.

Even now, when I have been doing this for decades, I come across something I have been merely tolerating when there is no need to. Why do I keep the old stained, faded coffee mug (it is not that special) when I have lovely English china that I do not often use?

By using your best, whether it is crystal glasses, beautiful dishes and silver cutlery; expensive (but half-price) shoes or French perfume, you will be bathing yourself in what you deserve.

If you do not feel like you deserve to use those things, ask yourself why? Often it is us as women who feel like we should be making sacrifices (for what, I am not sure, my mum calls it the 'burnt chop syndrome').

If you are worried about an item getting damaged or dirtied, try and let that go. Why would you house an item if you never use it? It is hard sometimes, I know, but when you make decision... nothing bad happens. What a relief. And, every so often when something does get broken, well, at least that crystal glass lived a full life.

## Surround yourself with beauty

When I think of my dream home in my dream life, it is not only luxuriously decorated, but clean and tidy, with touches of beauty from fresh-cut flowers and stacks of glossy picture books.

This can easily be recreated and you do not have to spend a cent. You may have a few blooms or even a small branch that you can put in a vase, take a few books down from your bookshelf and make a table-scape with a candle, shell or pinecone depending on the season.

Our favourite five-star hotel has a fresh

floral fragrance piped through the lobby – it really is glorious (I found out it is a Ginger White Tea fragrance). To recreate this for myself, I light candles or infuse fragrant oils and open all our windows for a few hours each day when I am at home.

To me fresh air plus a beautiful home fragrance = luxury.

The main thing with my dream home which is inspired by five-star hotels and beautiful homes that I browse online, is that they are uncluttered, airy and have only the necessary elements for a room, and those elements are of a high quality.

When I say high quality, it does not need to be costly. I have some fabulous pieces from second hand stores – a lamp that was $20 and an old wooden cabinet which stores our DVDs which was $30 from a charity shop.

Do not discount charity stores either. It is like a fun lottery because you never know what you will find in there, plus, you are supporting a worthy cause.

Some of my favourite framed pictures I have had forever, since I was a child, and others were painted by family members. I have cushion covers that I have made myself at little monetary cost, just my creativity and time.

It is gathering around you the styles and colours that you love that makes the difference.

Inspire yourself daily with your own thoughts, the social media accounts you follow, the books you keep on your shelves and your flavour of beauty that you surround yourself with.

## Keep only what your future self would have in her beautiful home

Decluttering room by room, making those hard decisions to donate or throw out stuff that we do not necessarily dislike, but that really does not add to our life; those are the items I find most difficult to let go.

When I have done test areas where I have taken everything out, whether it is my closet, home office, makeup area or kitchen pantry, and then put only what I'd imagine in my dream home back, it looks amazing – so good!

Doing this can take time too, so you have to put some aside to tackle an area. I often find that when I am inspired by something, perhaps it is a paragraph in a book, someone's comment about decluttering their bedroom and now it feels so calm and relaxing to be in, or perhaps an Instagram post (Courtney Carver's *Be More with Less* always activates me in a gentle and inspiring way), it takes less effort to declutter.

I am powered with excitement and effortlessly sort through an area and make quick decisions about letting things go. There is no room in a life that you want to feel luxurious, expensive and cosseting for items such as:

*Clothing that mocks you*

*Gifts that make you feel bad*

*Books you haven't read but keep because you 'should'*

*Kitchen gadgets you thought would be great but they are such a pain to clean afterwards*

*Extra plastic containers, shoeboxes, fancy shopping bags and other storage containers that you've kept to put things in*

*Makeup that is not quite the right colour for you (your colouring is not going to change)*

*Shoes that pinch*

*Half-done craft projects that you've lost*

*enthusiasm for or the child is now grown (I often see these packaged up at charity shops, someone else would love to finish it, no guilt required for you)*

I am sure you can add your own list of items that do not belong in your five-star life. As you go through your things, ask yourself *Would my future self, the lady who lives in her beautiful home have this?* When I ask myself that, it becomes *Would the dream me have this, not-quite-right top with scratchy fabric and slightly-tight sleeves in her closet?* No, she would not!

Framing things this way makes it quick and easy to see what belongs in your dream life, and what does not.

## Visit five-star luxury and soak it in

Even when we earnt very little, my husband and I loved to feel luxurious and surround ourselves with the feeling of wealth, because we knew we would have that one day in our glittering future. One of our favourite ways to do this was stay at The Langham – our favourite five-star hotel in the city we lived in.

We also joined their loyalty scheme which

meant we received late checkout, a bottle of wine, an international newspaper of our choice, a fresh fruit platter and bottled water every time we stayed. We only stayed once or twice a year, but the cost for a night was so worth it because it kept us going and helped us look forward to a future that we dreamed of.

And because the hotel was in our city, there was no travel time or cost; we simply drove down the road. If you do not have a gorgeous hotel in your town, research a luxury bed and breakfast or perhaps a beach cottage. When I first suggested to my husband that we have an overnight mini-break in our own city, he was not agreeable at all; saying *I am not paying to stay somewhere when I can just go home instead,* but eventually I suppose I talked him into it (story of his life) and now he is a total convert.

We travelled to Sydney for a long weekend last year, and we were excited to see there was a Langham there. When we stay one night in Auckland the price is not so bad, but staying four nights in a more expensive city meant the cost was a lot more than we wanted to spend. We booked a lovely serviced apartment instead.

One morning when we were leaving to go and find a nice place for breakfast after strolling the streets of Sydney, I said *Let's go to the*

*Langham for breakfast.* Because it was a last minute decision, it almost felt like we were playing hooky.

There were not many people in the restaurant because it was later on a Monday morning, so we had the glorious luxury buffet almost to ourselves, with fresh coffee and the Sydney newspapers spread out. Even though we did not want to spend all that money on staying at a five-star hotel, we got to enjoy a morning there at a quite reasonable price considering the fun we had.

Where is there a place near where you live that you can go for a meal or even a drink? Really make an outing out of it.

At our local Langham, I went in for a coffee one afternoon. It was a weekday, so there were plenty of tables in the beautiful atrium area and when my coffee arrived, it came with a little plate of cookies at no extra cost. Such a nice touch. The ambience was gorgeous, a *harpist* was playing for goodness sake and all for the same price as a coffee anywhere else.

I was *so* happy reading my book for half an hour with my five-star coffee. *How lucky am I?* I kept thinking to myself.

## Replace broken items with quality, cherish the rest.

To feel like I have a luxurious life, I do not need to have all new stuff. However, I do like what I use to be in good condition, of good quality and most importantly that it work well.

I used to buy the cheapest of whatever I needed at the time, whether it was a vacuum cleaner or a set or sheets; but now I see the value in shopping less and buying better quality when I do need something. I probably spend the same amount of money overall, but it feels so, so different.

If something is damaged or cannot be cleaned, I will get rid of it. Then I can decide if I want to replace it, and what with. Aside from those occasions, I take great pleasure from the items in my home which help make my life easier and more pleasurable. I love functional, useful, well-made items.

I keep my possessions clean and in good order and I do not keep them for best. Things are meant to be used! It took me a while to learn that and now I can honestly say I do not keep anything for best - if I want to use it, I will.

Most nights, I serve my sparkling water in a champagne flute. Regularly, I will have coffee from my small collection (less than a handful of pieces) of inherited vintage English china. And often we eat from my late nana's dinner-set which I love (English 'Belle Fiore'), along with our silver cutlery. The cutlery needs to be hand-washed rather than put in the dishwasher but I do not mind.

In Ralph Lauren's self-written book, he talks about how as a young man with not a lot of money he preferred utilitarian items such as an army surplus jacket or an old wooden piece of furniture – items that are made honestly with good quality materials in a superior way which means they are going to last a long time.

I feel this way too and it takes me back to the thought of investing in quality, which does not necessarily mean expensive (not all the time anyway). To enjoy using and looking after items I have come by in the past, and be selective about what I allow into my life in the future, I remember Ralph's basic tenets:

*Looking after your possessions, caring for them and showing them respect*

*Keeping something for a long time and mending or fixing if need be*

*Gathering furniture and clothing over time to create your own unique style*

*Aiming for style, not fashion.*

*Appreciating old and battered things, whether they are adorning the home or the body*

*Embracing utility items*

My family did not gift me with family heirlooms, so 95% of my furniture I have bought. I can think of two pieces that I brought with me when I left home and I still have them. I remember choosing them with my mother; they caught my eye then and I still love them now. Neither were expensive at all, however they are attractive, solid and functional – definitely built to last. I appreciate items made from real honest-to-goodness materials and I will continue to use and care for them.

With the items that surround you in your home, do you love and maintain them? Appreciate their authenticity and embrace their 'battle scars' from daily life. There is a difference between something that is damaged, and the patina that comes from everyday use.

I would always throw out a chipped dish,

however I love that our oiled wood hall table has a few marks here and there or a Persian-type rug that is getting softer in colour by the year, from the strong sun where we live.

## Feel luxurious in budget-friendly ways

In Estée Lauder's inspiring autobiography titled '*Estée – A Success Story*' she wrote about having anchors of the life she aspired to have. She had fresh cut flowers, gold ornaments and beautiful vases in her office. I know she was slightly self-serving in saying that, because she wanted ladies to buy her perfume as one of those luxurious touches, but it is such a great concept.

What can you have in your home to anchor in the feeling of expense and luxury? For me it is things like:

**Candles** – scented for during the day, then at night I light tea lights or unscented pillar candles. Candles can be so inexpensive for the ambience they give out. If you are not a fan of candles, there are LED tea lights which are safer when you have young children or don't like the fire risk.

And if you have a beautiful scented candle you have been given for a gift, light and enjoy it today. The aroma will fade over time, so you are not gaining anything by saving it up.

**Lamps** instead of overhead lights at night, whether it is in the living room or the bedroom. There are many gorgeous and inexpensive lamp styles available, and you can make more of a statement with a lamp because it is an accent piece in a room, much like a scarf on a classic outfit.

**Beautiful room scents** – in an oil infuser, plug-in scents, room sprays, incense every so often – I am such a perfume girl; I can never have too many nice smells, others are more sensitive so prefer less.

**Nice cushions on our sofa** – I have two soft, fluffy sheepskin cushion covers I love to display in winter, changing them for something more summery when it is hot. I love that the touches of white sheepskin make our home feel like a luxurious Aspen ski lodge.

**Always having a clean kitchen** – this is my husband's contribution when I asked him what he found luxurious at home. Putting items in the dishwasher during the day (I am so grateful our current home came with a dishwasher), doing the dishes straight after a meal, wiping the counters down and putting away items when you have used them means it is always a pleasure to walk into or past your kitchen.

**A beautifully made bed** – making our bed nicely every day makes such a difference; instantly the room looks better, and it brings about the feeling of my luxury lifestyle to have a serene hotel-like bedroom.

**Tissues and handcream** around the home – I have always had handcream all over the house because I love to look after my hands, but in recent times I have added nice quality tissues. When I was growing up we never had tissues around, so we would use a square of toilet paper to blow our nose, for example. As a result, I have this thought that tissues are extravagant, when they cost less than $2 for a box that lasts for ages!

So I started dotting tissues around the house – both bathrooms, my office and the living room. They are so handy and I love having them here. One day, my husband said *I love that whenever I need a tissue, there's one handy.* Men might not comment on every feminine touch around the house, but they always notice and appreciate them.

**Fresh towels often** – something I have started doing recently is changing my bath-towel more often. When you stay in a hotel, it is so luxurious to pull down a fresh towel from the stack. At home though, I made a towel last a week. I never really thought about it much, just changed my towel when I did the laundry.

Now, when I wash my hair (every two or three days), I use the old towel as a turban to keep my wet hair from dripping down me, and use a new towel to dry myself off. I then put the old towel in the wash. I am in love with my new practice. It feels so decadent and it is only 1-2 towels extra per week. I love the sense of abundance I feel from doing this and it costs very little.

**Cloth napkins at meal-times** – something I have done for many years is to use cloth napkins at dinnertime – every single night whether we have guests or not. Some were gifts from people who know we use them, some I bought, and some I made (they are an easy project).

They are easy to throw in the laundry basket after dinner and I do a hot soak wash once a week. We might not wash them every time, either. If they are pristine, I fold them for our next meal. Having a cloth napkin on your lap feels far more luxurious than having a roll of paper towels on the table, I can tell you!

**Clear surfaces** and clean rooms, which brings about a feeling of space. It is so easy to put things down and then they sit there for days. Clearing temporary items off the dining table, kitchen counter or coffee table instantly anchors in the feeling of peace and ease. It is amazing that something so simple can change the feeling of a room, and therefore you.

**Inspiring music** playing in the background – in fact, when I picture our fabulous future, there is always soft music playing, all day when I am at home; so, I do it now to bring that future to me.

**A 'comfort drawer'** in my bedside table. I got this idea from Colin Cowie, in his inspiring book *'Chic: the guide to life as it should be'*. Colin wondered why we would want all our detritus out on the nightstand top when we could have it neatly stored in the top drawer, thus keeping a pleasing and calm look to the room.

I tried this idea at once and have stuck with it for close to a decade. Before that, my bedside table top had a stack of books, lip balm, a pad and paper, hand cream and many other items I'm sure. Now all it has on top is a lamp and my current book.

In my top drawer, I have a few divider trays to keep everything tidy, keeping at my fingertips such items as:

My journals
Bookmarks
Handcream
Body butter
Lip balm
Pens and pencils
Pretty notepads
Lavender oil
Wheat eye bag

It is so nice to have my tidy drawer full of pretty girly things, and they are right at hand as I am relaxing in our bedroom and writing in my journal after dinner.

## Curate your wardrobe

When I was a champion shopper with a stuffed

closet, I was always looking around for the next new thing to buy. After I had my empty bank account/full closet epiphany, I changed my viewpoint and was happy to mix-and-match my current items to create new outfits and wear the same things over and over.

I started reading about the voluntary simplicity movement around the same time, and leading on from that was the minimalist movement. I knew I would never be a true minimalist though, as much as I enjoyed reading blog articles with empty rooms pictured (so peaceful looking).

From this study, however, I had found another way to look at having a smaller wardrobe of clothing.

Enter the *capsule collection*. It is a common enough phrase now, but back then it seemed so new and enticing. It made me think of a designer's runway collection where the pieces were different enough so they did not all look identical, but interlocked together in a way that gave you endless outfit possibilities.

Reframing how I viewed my closet from *I can't go shopping anymore because I have spent all my money* to *I am curating my capsule collection for the season* was revolutionary for me and it still is. I love that I only shop for a few items at the beginning of the season and then I am free to forget about shopping until the change of season six months later. It frees up so much time, energy, mental space and money for other areas.

As each season rolled around, I got rid of so-so items, and having these gone made my wardrobe feel like I had more. I felt more prosperous with less! Having fewer options also made it easier to remember what I had in my closet (nothing got lost at the back) and also to keep up with the laundry because I would start running out of clothes if I left it longer than a week.

Extra tip: to help avoid temptation from clothing sales, I unsubscribed from all shopping emails and only re-joined, or would browse their website to see if there were any good offers, when I needed something.

## Cultivate an expensive-looking personal style

Over the years I have torn out many magazine articles focusing on how one might look expensive and high-maintenance on a budget. I still love to read through them and they always inspire me.

One of my blog posts called '*How to look expensive*' is consistently in the top ten reader favourite posts of all time on my blog *howtobechic.com*, so it can't be just me who is interested in looking like an heiress, trust fund princess or European royal.

Personal style attributes that belong in my five-star life include:

*A light, golden tan - using facial bronzing powder with a light touch year-round, and self-tanner on my legs and arms in the summer.*

*Classic, simple clothing in rich-looking neutrals (black, navy, cream, white, grey, camel, tan). Yes, you can tell some expensive clothing, but you can just as easily build a wardrobe that looks expensive which did not cost a lot.*

*Restrained, classic jewellery with a statement piece every once in a while – no-one has to know that my half-carat diamond studs are cubic zirconias.*

*Mostly solid colours – very few prints, perhaps the odd stripe*

*Immaculate grooming – smooth, moisturised*

*legs, filed polished nails, cared for feet, buffed skin, natural looking makeup and healthy hair in a natural shade.*

*Big sunglasses, which always look glamorous and rich to me.*

This list is my own personal style, yours may look different. No matter the type of clothing you love to wear, good grooming is key to the rich look and the great thing about the items on this list is that none of them need to cost much. It is all about effort and intention.

## Have an elegant personal demeanour

Well-to-do people often have an aura of ease and elegance around them. They are not trying to impress you (if they are, they may not be rich, just heavily mortgaged – the classic 'wannabe' scenario). One of my wealthiest friends always looks immaculate and you can tell she is certainly not poor, however she plays it down and never talks about money or possessions. She always asks questions and would rather talk about you than her.

How can we cultivate that ease around ourselves? I believe it comes with confidence and kindness. Of course it is easy to feel good when you do not have any money worries, but having a lot of money does not insulate you from everything in life. There are still health issues, family dramas, daily issues to deal with and that age old *What are we going to have for dinner?* decision.

Having confidence and kindness is easy to cultivate on your way to having money, and in fact it helps you arrive at being that person. If you have an image in mind of how you might be different when you have less money stress, try being that person now.

Be that person who has all the time in the world so does not feel rushed. Be that person who happily spritzes on her best perfume because she knows it will not be her last bottle ever. These things may sound minor, but it is all the little things we do every day that add up to who we are becoming.

You are creating your future dream life (or not) based on all the decisions you make, every single day. Who you are being today is who you will be five, ten, twenty years from now.

It is not always easy. I can still fall back into my old way of thinking every so often where I will say to myself *I want to be elegant and chic, slim and stylish. I know I will be like that one day, but today I just feel like slouching around in my PJs eating chocolate before lunch and watching reality television.* When I have done this I have felt bad inside (and not just from the chocolate overload) because I know I am going against what I really want.

It does not mean you have to be a perfect superwoman all the time; it just means to look at what you want in the future and then take steps towards that now.

If I slob out and eat badly now, I can see down the track I will still be that person, just older and in worse health with less motivation. That is not the vision I have for my future self.

## 'Expensive' décor on a budget

As with personal style, I love to research ways to make our home look more luxe and rich without spending a lot of money. An online article I read about a woman who had her home shown in a magazine, said the main reason why the homes in magazines look so good is because they have been decluttered and cleaned to within an inch of their life. Plus, they tape lamp cords to table legs. But mostly it is decluttering, decluttering, decluttering and cleaning, cleaning, cleaning! Of course you probably will have a rather nice home to be asked to feature in a magazine in the first place, but a dirty dusty living room, no matter how fancy the furnishings are, will still not look good.

Ask yourself of your master bedroom or living room for example, how could you make this room look more luxe in your style? What could you add... or take away? Often it is something taken away that opens up more space and gives a luxurious feeling.

Decorate with pieces and colours you associate with richness. For me, it is gorgeous over-size sofas in a luxurious neutral fabric, thick drapey curtains and warm, golden/black tones with low lighting.

Something else I adore is short, dense, plush, velvety carpet and I know in our next home we will have a carpet like that. It hushes footsteps and seems so luxe. Perhaps with some marble tiles at the entrance way? Delicious.

I have a list which is my inspiration board for our home style. I change components of it every so often (mainly when I see something new that I love) but overall, it has changed little over time. It is a fluid concept and helps me make good decisions.

*Lacquered black, cream, warm rich, ochre,*

*touches of deep red*
*Gilt/gold and oiled wood*
*Soft white/cream/sacking/linen*
*Peaceful haven, calm sanctuary*
*Plush, golden light*
*An oasis of calm*
*Ordered, organized, attractive*
*Natural materials – wood, wrought iron, wool, cotton, wicker*
*Candlelight*
*Fresh, fragrant, floral air*
*Elegant casual*
*Casual glamour*
*Authentic, genuine*
*Hotel chic*
*Spare sophistication*
*Rustic elegance*
*Sophisticated chic*
*Luxuriously simple*
*Rustic luxe*
*Black or copper iron chandelier with dimmer*
*Sparse and spare Parisian chic*
*Big open spaces to breathe*
*A place for everything to live*
*Even utility items/areas are attractive to look at – pared down essentials in square, flat-woven baskets*
*Clean and fresh smelling*

*Replace/repair damaged or dirty items*
*Orderly and sparse, stylish, chic and sophisticated*
*Calming neutral colours*
*Feels light and airy inside*
*Regular decluttering of items that others can gain use from*

Why not start your own vision for your ideal home décor? Include any little detail that makes you feel luxurious, wealthy and brings about an aura of richness; then use this as a blueprint for what you bring into your home and also what you let go of.

Declutter anything that makes you feel poor or low-budget. One thing I can think of straight away is a set of plastic drawers I bought to house goodness knows what. At the time it was my knitting yarns, some of which I had bought, but many I had inherited from my grandmother-in-law.

Over time I decluttered the acrylic yarns and colours I did not like, so I actually do not need an ugly four-drawer tower of plastic for my collection of wool, which has shrunk away to a core of gorgeous yarns that fit in one container.

I still have that plastic drawer set and it makes me feel low-rent – like I cannot afford wooden drawers for my clothes. It is hard to donate something still in perfect order that I am sure I could find some use for, but it is not something that belongs in my dream-life home.

The alternative is to re-purpose it into a laundry or garage where it would be more appropriate than my home office where I can see it as I write.

# Chapter 4.

## *See how you rich are already*

Even if you do not feel particularly well off, the simple fact that you have a roof over your head and the possessions that you do, makes you wealthier than a large percentage of the world's population. Having been born where you were, was a great bonus that came about from the lottery of your birth.

Still, despite knowing this deep down, it is easy to get all 'spoilt brat' about it and want more, more, more. This does not help us feel any better and in fact is counter-productive. Of course you already know that, but knowing it does not often help either!

Getting your mind into a good feeling state, by looking at all the ways you are abundant right now works wonders. In this chapter, I share some of my favourite ways of getting into a positive mindset about money; this then spills over into your actions and you will find over time you are becoming a different, more prosperous person.

## Know where your finances are at

Feeling organized and on top of things helps any situation, especially your money life. I used to know someone who filed their bank statements in a shoebox in the closet – unopened. There were years' worth in there and it used to boggle me – just how could you know what was happening if you did not even look? It was before Internet banking too, so there was no other way this person could have kept their bank accounts up to date.

I know if you are in debt or barely keeping your head above water, it will not seem like a fun night in to have a filing and budgeting party, but it is only hard once – the first time. After that it is simply a matter of opening envelopes (or emails) as they come in.

I have always used a ring binder folder with a set of dividers inside. One divider can be for each bank account statement, one for the power bill, one for the phone bill etc. My folder is getting less use now that we have many bills sent by email or available to view online. I do not print them out, but I do open them as soon as they come in and enter the date and direct debit amount on my banking spreadsheet.

Before the spreadsheet I used a paper diary, but the principle is the same. I have the dates when my pay comes in, and I note all the outgoing payments between paydays so I know how much money I have to leave in that account to cover all the payments.

I transfer the balance to our savings and some of that is used to pay our Visa in full each month (we use our Visa for all daily expenses). For some, the Visa method may not work; for example, if you cannot resist impulse purchases. In that case you may wish to use a debit card or an all-cash system.

Most deposits and payments are automated. When we start a new account with someone, say we have changed electricity companies, I set up a direct debit payment straight away; that way I do not have to worry about paying the bill manually.

I check our bank accounts daily, and it is easy because of this. It is one of the things I routinely check when I am on the computer in the morning. Whenever I leave things for a few days, it gets harder. If I am busy or unmotivated it is tough to catch up, but I do it because I know it feels better when I am done. I really do feel physically better knowing that everything is in order.

You might be wondering just where can you get motivation from, if you are in debt and do not want to look at the numbers. Think about it this way. Do you want to get out of debt or do you want to sink down further? Do you want to improve your relationship with money, so that you can be better off financially in the future? It's a simple choice and only you can make it.

This is the first step. It might not be a pretty picture, but you can only improve from there. It is like facing the scales after a long time of burying your head in the sand and eating everything in sight. It is shocking, but necessary.

And here is the exciting part – you can make a plan to pay off debts and then, start your saving and investment plans. Once you know how deep the hole is, you can start filling it in, and then, building your mountain.

Spreadsheets are great for this because you

can make a forecast by noting down future payments and seeing when your debt will be gone. Then you tweak the payments up by $10 a week and see that you could be debt-free a few months earlier. $10 a week is easy – it is a work lunch or coffee and a muffin!

I get really motivated when I can see how things are going to turn out; and if you plan a strategy and then follow it each week, you will find yourself on a great financial path and feeling *amazing* about it.

## Speak positively about your finances

It is really important to speak positively, both the thoughts in your head and when you speak out loud around other people. Saying 'I can't afford this' puts a downer on things, and it probably is not even true. You could probably afford a lot more than you think, but you choose to spend your money in other ways.

Let me illustrate it like this: I could afford a Ferrari if I wanted to. But how? Easy, I could choose to buy a Ferrari if I sold my house. I would have to live in the Ferrari (quite a cram with my husband and two cats), but that is a choice we could make. I could technically afford a Ferrari. I could also afford a fancy boat if I wanted to (only I would have to sell the Ferrari and live on the boat instead).

Everything is a choice. The obvious (and my) choice is that I would rather have a house (and I do not really desire a Ferrari or a boat, they are just examples); but what I am showing you is that you could likely afford whatever it is you think you cannot. It's just that you would rather spend that same money on something else.

Rather than thinking you cannot afford something, you are simply prioritising your spending on other things. You are choosing not to buy that item at this time (or ever) because you place more value on other purchases or investments.

It really makes such a difference that you say this to yourself, and because your mind is taking in everything you say, you will probably find you start having better financial 'luck'. Your mindset may improve in other areas too.

I truly believe that if you can imagine a goal, hold it in your mind, focus on it and take action steps, you can achieve it. When I have family members ask me about my plans sometimes, I often hold back on what I tell them, because in the past they've looked at me like I was crazy and I can see how it must look to them.

But I also know what I believe, and I choose to believe that I can achieve whatever I desire; the dream lifestyle where I write from home, our quiet house in the country, all of it.

And it starts with thinking and speaking positively both about your current situation, and what you want to happen in the future. There are truly no limitations to this.

## Cultivate a happy and relaxed feeling around money

This tip goes along with speaking positively about your finances. In the past (and I still do it sometimes now, until I check myself) I would have the following feelings about money coming in or going out:

(about money coming in, perhaps my pay packet)
*That is not much, it won't last until next month, others are paid better, etc.*

(about money going out, say I have just opened our electricity bill)
*Wow, so expensive, those big companies are ripping us off, what can we do though, we are helpless, etc.*

Do I sound empowered and happy about my situation? No! Things have changed a lot for me financially and of course it is down to a lot of different things, but I believe one of those things is feeling happy and relaxed about the flow of money into and out of my life.

I understand it might not be easy to change the way you feel when things are tight, however look at it this way. Money will always be coming in and going out, like waves on a beach.

Whenever you receive money, whether it is from your pay packet, a birthday present, finding a coin on the ground, always say *Thank you*. I say *Thank you, Universe* or just plain *Thank you* spoken to myself. It feels far better than the automatic thought of *That is not much,* and it trains your mind to feel good.

Whenever you are paying out money, as with my electricity bill example, think to yourself *Thank you for trusting me to pay this bill*, or simply give thanks for that service. At the supermarket where I seem to spend *so* much money and our household is just two people and two cats, I think *Thank you for the ease and convenience of buying our groceries* as I pay.

This might sound a bit airy fairy for you, but maybe just try it and see if it helps you feel better. If it does, excellent. Feeling good is one of the main ways you create good stuff in your life.

Do not make things hard for yourself. Know that life is more fun when you are not struggling, and life does not have to be hard; we make it that way sometimes! Know that everything will work out fine and that the universe always has your back, because it does.

I am sure there have been situations in your life, where at the time you thought things were falling apart, but now that you look back things actually turned out better. I have certainly had those times, and of course sometimes there are tragedies which have no goodness at all; but for the most part, things always work out for the best. Therefore, in the future you can trust that this will be the case as well.

## Contentment as a financial tool

I know it may sound strange to say that 'contentment' is a fantastic financial tool, but it really is. I love the saying that goes '*happiness is not having what you want, but wanting what you have*'.

When you appreciate what you have, look after it and value it, you are more content. When you are content, you are not chasing the next big thing. When you are content you are not looking outside yourself (and into a mall) for happiness. Life opens up in so many ways when you develop a deep contentedness of all the wonderful things you already have in your life.

'Count your blessings' sounds so twee and clichéd, but it has been around forever for good reason. When we are focusing on all the good in our life we feel much better about ourselves and our situation, which means we are not chasing shiny new things to brighten ourselves up. We are bright from within!

Next time you feel the urge to shop for no reason, stand still for a moment and ask yourself why. For me, it is that I am avoiding housework because it is boring and tiring, or maybe I just feel like something new to perk myself up.

If I am at work and I think I would like to go out for a break to browse around, I know it is because I have some jobs to do that I am putting off. But going out shopping is not going to get them done. Ultimately it will feel far better to tackle that job, even if I do not finish it that day, than to ignore it completely and have the guilt hanging over me. And I will still have to do it at some stage.

I used to let boring, low-importance tasks build up in my in-tray and there was a permanent little cloud of doom like in Charlie Brown hanging over me. The cloud was not very big, but it was always there.

Once I made the decision to have my tray cleared everything changed. I had a big blow-out one day where I went through everything, and now there are a few folders with pending jobs I need to keep out to follow-up. Anything that lands on top I deal with straight away. It is a marvelous feeling.

If I am at home and feel like I need to escape the house; like I said above, it is because my house needs a good clean and tidy. If I just tell myself what to do, like I am a child (being my own chic mentor), I will just start putting things away, polishing the coffee table, decluttering an area, doing a load of laundry and things fall into place.

I feel more grounded and calmer; our home looks and feels better; I have not gone out and needlessly spent money on 'stuff' and the sense of satisfaction is immense. That passing feeling of needing to escape is gone; it was only a transient thought that I did not need to act on.

Remembering that everything I need is already with me, not in a shop, helps me feel more content with my life; plus, feeling content with my life helps get me into action. It is a wonderful two-way street.

## Think beyond a purchase to its exit

Occasionally I hanker after something new and shiny; for example, I might be walking through an inexpensive homeware store and see lovely coffee mugs which I know are the coffee mugs of my minimalist home dreams. However, when I actually imagine buying six or eight of them and taking them home, there would be no room for them.

Our narrow coffee mug shelves are already full, so I have to ask myself if am I willing to donate perfectly good coffee mugs which I love, simply to accommodate a newer version? It is one thing to replace an item because it is worn out or broken, but to replace items simply because you have found something else you like better, well, that does not feel like my ideal simple life to me. Instead, I can simply think *We do not need coffee mugs, but aren't those ones gorgeous?* and leave them on the shelf.

Buying them would also be not a considered choice. I did not leave the house that morning with 'new coffee mugs' on my shopping list; no, I simply saw them and wanted them. That is where I used to miss the link; I would buy the mugs and then declutter the old ones. But where's the point in that?

Thinking beyond a purchase to its exit is such a useful tool to keep in one's *Financially Chic* toolkit – it works with anything. I love the colourful crispness of new magazines, however I know I find it hard to part with them and then the stacks stress me out. It is far better for me to buy one or two titles that I really love and know I will re-read, and borrow the rest from the library, or, go without. They are only a passing fancy when I am in the bookstore.

Another angle of thinking beyond the purchase is when buying clothing. I might love the look of a new white shirt, or a dramatic top in a light shade; however, I know from prior experience that because I always put body cream on my neck and décolletage, any white collar seems to turn yellow within a short time. Hot bleach washes, scrubbing with laundry soap, nothing seems to work.

So, I make life simple and do not buy these items for myself anymore. Again, I admire them on others and choose differently for myself, so that I can live the simple and stress-free life of my dreams.

# Chapter 5.
## *Inspire yourself to a wealthy future*

A fantastic question to ask yourself is *How would I imagine myself living, if money was no object?* If you could dream up your future with a million dollars in the bank, how would you spend your time and what kind of things would you have around you?

And then ask yourself, how can I bring those things into my life right now? Drawing towards you all the ways you will be when you have more money is very powerful. You are living as if you are that person now, and this can make things change rapidly.

When I wrote down all the details that would make me feel like I was living a life of privilege, I realised that almost all of the things on my list I could start doing straight away – so I did. What a revelation that was.

Things such as:

**Having long, silky blow-dried hair**. Maybe I was not going to a salon to have it done, like someone with more money would; but I could decide to make more of an effort with my hair (because I am pretty 'relaxed' about it often, I hate to admit), taking the time to dry it properly when I washed it. It is not that I do not have the extra half an hour it needs – I am just lazy!

**Fresh cut flowers**. Occasionally I buy them now, and I also pick flowers and fern from our garden to put in bud vases. I also love my silk flowers which I move around the home every so often. I know some people do not like artificial flowers but if you can find higher quality ones, they are gorgeous. And make sure you keep them clean. I swish mine around in warm soapy water every once in a while, or you can 'dust' them with a hairdryer on cool setting.

**Learn to practice meditation**. I could totally do this now if I really wanted to, no need to wait until I was 'rich', but still, I do not. I think it is on my list because I feel like I don't have time to explore these things right now, but isn't that funny – no time to learn how to meditate, when it probably gives you more time because it changes the way you relate to time. Untangling these thoughts helps me realise it is *not* about having more time/more money. I need to look at how I speak to myself (such as my underlying thoughts of *I do not have time for this!*)

I also wrote out what my first-class life would look like. It is not fancy and jet set, but it sounds perfect to me. That is what I had to figure out too – I used to think that an expensive life meant fancy meals out and dry-clean only clothes, but for me, my five-star life includes an abundance of *space* and *freedom* instead. That sounds blissful.

My ideal rich girl life:

- Being a successful published author who works from her beautiful home office

- Having the time to read the books I own, enjoying them and getting value and inspiration from them
- Early bedtime routine – five minutes of yoga, relaxing, reading and journaling
- Gardening and pottering for pleasure
- Playing around in my sewing room
- Creating my bespoke capsule wardrobe
- Knitting for enjoyment and creation
- Deep breathing, stretches and relaxation
- Travel with my husband
- Have help around the house
- Fresh-cut flowers
- A beautifully furnished high-quality home
- A marble bathroom with all my skincare, makeup and perfume
- Land around us outside, so that we do not see any neighbours
- Mature trees and a beautiful easy-care garden
- Rescue cats and dogs who live a wonderful life with us

The crazy thing is, a lot of these things I can have right now. How fascinating is that? I am living a rich life already, and by doing more of the things I love, I can feel even richer (in all senses of the word) and more fulfilled.

What does your ideal rich life look like?

## Keep your vibration high

Having a high vibration (or frequency) is my biggest tip in feeling like a million dollars, even if you do not have much in the bank right now. But what does having a high frequency mean, and just how do you do it?

Basically it is about identifying what makes you feel good, and what does not. Activities such as overeating might feel good at the time because of the taste and enjoyment, but afterwards you do not feel so good because you have ended up with a stomach-ache; and especially after that, the not-good feeling continues because you have likely put on weight as a result (if you do it regularly, like I used to).

Identifying something as high frequency or low frequency helps you to make better choices. I read a quote that said motivation is like a lamp and you need to keep putting oil in it to keep it going, and I do think this is true. You constantly need to remember your goals and what you want, otherwise the old familiar and cozy habits sneak in again.

Another concept I love talks about an *easy* life versus a *successful* life. The old and familiar habits route is part of an easy life because it requires no effort. A successful life feels much better, but it requires intention. Most people choose the first option because it is automatic and you don't have to think too much about it; but I am not most people, I want a successful life. If you are reading this, I am sure you are the second type as well.

To identify frequency, it was helpful to make a list of my high/low frequency comparisons. I would ask myself if something felt good and then I would know what heading it went under – so simple. As I mentioned above, I might feel good whilst eating a whole large bar of Cadbury chocolate at once, but afterwards? Not so good.

This is such an illuminating exercise and provides you with great information, so I encourage you to start your own high/low frequency lists. If you have an entry for one, you can take the opposite and put it in the other to compile that list (it does not matter which side you start with).

## *High frequency*

*Three meals a day full of nutrients*

*Having non-screen (computer or television) down-time after dinner - reading, washing my face, journaling*

*Reading uplifting material online - blogs and Facebook of positive people*

*Positivity, looking for the good, smiling*

*Exquisite posture, my head being pulled up by an invisible thread, breathing fully*

*Movement using both big and small muscles*

*A neat and tidy home that is clean and with feminine decor touches*

*Keeping my wardrobe edited, making tailored adjustments as necessary*

*Washing and blow-drying my hair mostly every second day, occasionally every third*

*Creating my own inspiration/writing*

*Regular organizing and decluttering*

## *Low frequency*

*Indiscriminate snacking/junk foods/snacking in general*

*Being on the computer or watching television right up until bedtime*

*Reading the news online*

*Slumping, slouching, nit-picking, complaining, shallow breathing*

*Flomping down on the sofa, not using small muscles*

*Not doing housework or just doing the bare minimum, not changing display areas, leaving them to get dusty*

*Not blow-drying my hair and letting it go into a kinky and shapeless frizz then tying it back to try and hide that (which does not hide it at all)*

*Only taking in others' information and not creating my own*

*Not being organized at home, letting things pile*

*up all around so that I forget where things are*

How much nicer is the first list to read? The energy is lighter and you feel uplifted. Compare this to the feeling you get from reading the second list and you will get exactly what I mean about the feeling of high or low frequencies.

Reading through the first list when I am feeling lazy/snacky really helps lift my energy and get me back onto a good track.

## Share your dreams with your other half

If you are in a relationship, it is crucial that you are both on the same page about money and future goals. It is harder to stay focused on your goals, saving money, keeping your vibration high and developing your wealth consciousness if your spouse is negative and spending like there is no tomorrow. You will be pulling against each other and it will seem like hard work to get anywhere.

Nagging will not help, so forget that. What does work is to lead by example. Upgrade your financial knowledge by reading books and listening to inspiring audios and YouTube videos. I do all these things for myself only, but I know my husband listens in from time to time and sometimes he tells *me* about things that I know he must have picked up from something I was studying!

Another great tip is to include your spouse in your plans and dreams. Let them know what you would love to do with your life; what you imagine you would do if money was no object, and ask them similar questions. When we did buy lottery tickets every so often, from the time we bought the ticket until the time we found out we had not won, we would have the best fun dreaming of what we would do with the winnings.

We decided we would sell our business and move to a country property in a small town, to live a simple and peaceful life with plenty of time for our creative pursuits and each other. Lo and behold, we did not need to win the lottery for that; we are planning for it right now. And it all started with a dream and a conversation.

When you are out on a date night, relaxing on the sofa or driving somewhere together, ask questions such as:

*If you were 20 again, what career would you choose, knowing what you know now?*

*What would you do for a job if you could flick*

*the switch overnight and be in that role instantly?*

*If we won the lottery, how would we live our dream life? Would we still live in the town we do? Where could we move to?*

*What were your favourite things to do as a kid?*

Of course, you would not ask all these questions at once, but choosing one and seeing where the conversation goes is a fantastic way to open up the dream channels. This is how my husband and I first started talking about moving out of the city, and now we are doing it.

Be a shining example of positivity, hope, dreams, wishes and your fantasy future life. Know that anything is possible and that it is up to you to lead the way. Be encouraging and uplifting; their dream might not be your dream but it does not matter.

Just because men seem tougher and stronger than women, does not mean they do not have a fragile interior. They might feel uncertain about sharing their deepest desires. Women have been brought up to talk about these things; men often have not.

Be gentle on your other half and show

FIONA FERRIS

support for all their dreams, no matter how silly or inconsequential you may think they are. If you want him to continue to share and be open with you, you have to earn his trust. Do not share his stuff with other people either. Let him know he is safe to talk freely with you.

## Commit to being debt-free

Can you picture a life where you are free from monetary debt? Just take a moment to imagine the freedom that would provide, and feel the relief of being free and clear of any debt. Nothing hanging over your head. No more repayments to make. All the money that you earn you can take to live on and invest for your wealthy future.

It is not just a pipe dream, it is possible; and with freedom from debt comes an opportunity to live a different life if you desire it. You no longer work in a job you do not enjoy simply for the money. You could choose to work part-time instead. You could travel more, relax on the weekends instead of worrying about the bills. How amazing would that be?

When you have no debt, there are so many more choices. When I was younger and just starting out, it seemed great that you could have something straight away and pay it off; but that is how many of us get sucked into consumer debt, either with '3 years interest-free' (never mind all those hidden charges) or via credit cards. Consumer debt is bad news.

There are two kinds of debt: good debt and bad debt. If you have not heard these distinctions already, here is a brief recap:

*Good debt*

Many people consider 'good debt' to be debt on income-producing assets only, such as an investment property or a business. I would also classify good debt to be debt on appreciating assets such as your home and your education (within reason).

Still, you will want to pay any debt off – good or bad – as soon as possible. Compounding interest that is so beneficial to your savings and investments is equally effective, but in the opposite – detrimental – direction when it is applied to debt you are paying off.

*Bad debt*

Any form of consumer debt is 'bad debt', which

includes credit card spending, hire purchase, buying a car with payments and those sorts of things. The kinds of things you buy with bad debt *depreciate* (go down) in value, rather than *appreciate* (go up).

*Do not go into bad debt ever* is my advice on bad debt. Save up for those things instead. If you already have bad debt, pay it off as quick as possible – make it your life's priority and go at it like your hair is on fire (love that saying!) – because bad debt almost always has a much higher interest rate than good debt.

There are some finance gurus who say *Be debt-free, make it your first priority to clear all debt,* and other finance gurus who say *Never be debt-free, always have good debt so that you are leveraged.* I am in the middle on this, and for me, I choose to not have debt personally, however if we decide to trial owning a residential rental property (which we are seriously thinking about), we will have debt on that, but it will ideally be self-funding i.e. the rent will cover the mortgage.

Make a list of all your debts. Put all your good debts together on one list, and your bad debts together on another list. After making sure you are covering the minimum payments on all of your debts so that they not incurring penalty costs, look at your bad debt list.

Common sense would say to pay the highest interest rate debt off first, then move to the next highest interest rate debt. While I do agree you cannot go wrong if you choose this way, there is also a small tweak I would suggest.

If you have some quite small debts, no matter the interest rate, get rid of them first. I believe doing this will give you a sense of achievement and help you feel like you are actually getting somewhere – you are gaining traction.

Once these small amounts are repaid in full, focus on the highest interest rate debt on your bad debt list. Continue to pay the minimum payments, and add the amounts you were paying on the debts that are now cleared. This is called the *snowball method*: payments are getting bigger and bigger as you chew threw those pesky debts and it gets easier and easier to knock them out as the snowball grows.

Imagine the sense of satisfaction you will feel once all the bad debts are gone and you can focus on your good debts. I can tell you from experience – it feels like nothing else on earth. Suddenly our wages were our own and we had the extremely unusual feeling of *What can we invest our money in now?*

I want that same glorious feeling for you, and I know you can achieve it. Most people stick their head in the sand and trust that banks have their best interests at heart. Banks do not have your best interests at heart. They want you to be a long-term source of profit for their shareholders. How else do you think banks earn billions of dollars each year?

## Take inspiration from expensive stores

On my list of chic mentors, I do not just have people, I also have a handful of retail stores (even though I am not big on shopping). Retail stores spend a lot of time, money and expertise in creating a compelling feeling of wanting to buy into the lifestyle they offer. Ralph Lauren is a master at this.

What really draws me to a room, whether it is a hotel lobby, page in a magazine or an image online, is if it looks expensive and luxe. Over time I have come to see many similarities in what I am enticed by and I have used these to make our home look more luxurious on a small budget.

There is one very expensive furniture and home décor store in the city where I live. It is so expensive that it is mostly where the rich-listers shop.

One of my favourite ways to feel inspired is to dress nicely, treat myself to a coffee nearby and browse this store. I soak in the atmosphere, the music they are playing and generally take in all the details. I see what colours they use and find ideas for table-scapes. It does not matter that our coffee table costs less than a placemat in this store, I can still borrow inspiration to recreate their displays at home.

High-end stores are often bright and airy, with not so much stock that they look crammed. The music is elegant and stylish, perhaps a string concerto or something more modern such as a relaxed tempo European electronica mix.

When I get home, I am full of renewed inspiration to tweak our décor and see what I can add to our look. Often all my home needs is a good clean and tidy, which always makes any room look better.

## Read inspirational money books and find fun ways to educate yourself

Back when I worked as a secretary for a financial planning company, there were many books on money around the office. I quickly found out that they weren't all the same. Some were very dry and wordy textbook type publications, and then there were the personal finance books that were geared toward the customer, so they spoke in layman's terms.

Even some of those were very dull and boring. But a few caught my imagination and I found that they were often written by women and were not exclusively about finances. They often had an holistic approach, so they incorporated money, home, family, career, retirement; everything to do with living your life.

I read these quickly and with enthusiasm, and found a whole new world opening up to me. Maybe some families talk about money, investing and savings, but I do not recall these topics ever being discussed at my house. My dad had a business, my mum ran the home and my siblings and I went to school – nothing really crossed over. We never really talked about money and I am sure my family is not an anomaly.

From what others say, they had to learn about money themselves growing up (often the hard way). In addition, there is nothing really on these topics that is taught in schools either. This is a crazy situation, considering how money and finance touches everyone's life, whether you are a stay at home mother, corporate CEO, retail assistant or small business owner.

That is why I believe it is so important to educate yourself, no matter your age. The trick to making it interesting is to find money books that are on your wavelength. You can do this by looking through the personal finance display at a bookstore, your local library, or browsing Amazon.

If a book piques your interest, take a look inside. Read a few pages of a random chapter and see if it grabs you. If not, put it back and try another one. On Amazon you can read reviews, and often the top reviewers summarise the content of a book. This is useful on two levels. Firstly, you may find out some great tips to start with, and secondly you will get a feel for the book to see if you will like it.

One of my favourite books on money is '*The Millionaire Next Door*' by Thomas Stanley and William Danko. I read this book many years ago and have re-read it periodically as well as the follow-up book '*Stop Acting Rich*'.

The simple premise of '*The Millionaire Next Door*' is that the normal looking couple in the house next to yours could be millionaires. You may not be able to tell by looking at them because they drive normal cars, wear not especially fancy clothing and their house is not a palace. They do not wear Rolexes and they may run their own business.

If you see someone who is flashy and glitzy driving past in their Rolls Royce, they are likely to be either seriously wealthy and enjoying the fruits of their efforts, or someone who wants to give off the appearance of being rich but in actuality is drowning in debt behind the scenes.

What this book gives me permission to do, is *be myself*. It is okay if I no longer desire a fancy car and am content with my Toyota. It is okay if I am a casual dresser who has very few formal outfits in her closet. It is so refreshing to know that I can be exactly as I am *and* wealthy – no airs and graces necessary.

Here are a few of my other favourite books on money:

'*The Richest Man in Babylon*' by George S. Clason
'*Get Rich Lucky Bitch*' by Denise Duffield-Thomas
'*Retire Young, Retire Rich*' by Robert Kiyosaki

Any of Suze Orman, Jean Chatzky, Glinda Bridgforth and David Bach's books are great too.

I first came across all of these money writers when Oprah did her '*Debt Diet*' series several years ago. I loved that series, so if you can find any snippets on YouTube, do watch, they're great.

Another excellent place to build your money knowledge is in your local newspaper or online newspapers. I do not read the general news any longer; however, I love to read the business, personal finance or money sections. There are often interesting articles, helpful tips and useful information. At the very least, I am absorbing things and perhaps learning something.

One of my favourite local writers is Mary Holm at nzherald.co.nz. She answers readers' questions and it is amazing how often they are relevant to my situation.

A lady came into our store once who looked a lot like the picture of Mary in the paper. My heart started beating and I wondered if I should ask her if she was Mary. It was hard to tell from the thumbnail picture online if it was her or not. Thankfully I did not ask, because when she paid for her purchase, I saw the name on her debit card and it wasn't her. Phew, embarrassment and crazy fan moment avoided!

## Think as if you were creating your own personal brand

A really fun project to do is actually cultivate your own personal brand. What would your new prosperous self's way of life look like? In a notebook, write out what you would like people to associate with you as a person. Also write down others who inspire you and think about what characteristics they possess that you most admire.

Write down how you want your home and wardrobe to look, then bring it all together into a personal brand. Your favourite colours to wear and decorate with could even become your 'brand' colours so that people get a consistent message from you.

Have a few keywords or phrases which exemplify the feeling you are going for. For me, I would say:

*A simple life*
*Kindness to people and animals*
*Enchantment and fun*
*Elegant neutral colours*
*Elevating the everyday*
*Luxurious simplicity*

Dreaming about things like this brings them into your life because it puts those things in your mind, and you then end up taking action on them. It is much like saying to yourself 'what is blue in this room?' and looking around you. You cannot help but notice everything that is blue.

What this is doing is training your mind to notice the things you want in your life, and your mind obliges. That is why it is *so* important to shift your focus away from those things you do not want in your life because the same will happen.

Others respond to all these things because you are cohesive – you are not a fairy goddess one day and French Chic pencil skirt the next; you are not wearing real fur one day and volunteering at the animal shelter the next. It does not matter if your brand is a blend of different styles, it just matters that it is what you love and that you are consistent. Consistency builds trust. You will create your own unique blend of style by doing this, and no-one else will be the same.

You may wonder what having a personal brand has to do with money and success. To me it is all part of knowing what you want your future to look like, so that you can take steps towards it. Thinking through your personal brand is just another way to bring clarity to your vision.

It is okay to be inspired by others even if you feel like you are copying them at first. It is not exactly copying; you are just trying on different ways of being for size. If you are true to what feels good to you, you will either keep them or let them go after a short while. Both are a good outcome. Everything you 'keep' is building together to become your own brand – 'You Inc'!

It is part of going through life that we will be influenced by others. What we take on shapes us and also influences those who are watching us. We are all artists in our own way, even those who say they are not the artistic type. Just living your life is an art form. Maybe your art form is very simple and routine and you do not feel it is that special, but it is, and it is all yours.

## Have role models

Having inspiring role models helps keep your head screwed on. It is most important to remember your goals and your big 'why', and having role models helps with this. Role models do not always have to be people in your real life; they can be celebrities or even movies and television programmes.

When the Bond movie *Spectre* came out, I was not that keen, but I went with my husband because I am an easy-going wife who wants to share experiences with her man. I had not really watched any James Bond movies in the past thinking of them as boy movies, but after seeing *Spectre* I am keen to view more.

*Spectre* had such a sexy and luxe vibe and even the fast cars were a thrill. Monica Belucci was divine and Lea Seydoux was fabulous. And as for Daniel Craig, he was not really on my radar before but now, wow, so hot. It is the way he holds himself and the way he dresses in the movie. And of course it was set in beautiful places and had breath-taking aerial shots, and scenes at incredible locations in London, Austria, Tangier/Morocco and Rome.

Watching something like this, is very inspiring to me to live a sexier, richer life, and by this I mean - elegant style, luxe surroundings, taking good care of yourself, beautiful posture etc.

I loved the lady characters and watched what they were wearing and how they held themselves, but it was really Daniel Craig that had the most effect on me. His posture was impeccable, he was in incredible shape and wore his skinny-cut suits well. Even his casual clothing was gorgeous. If I was a guy, I would definitely covet his look and my goodness, he was so masterful.

What did I take from Daniel Craig's Bond character?

*Owning your space in the world*

*Believing you are worth that space*

*Walking like you mean it*

*Dressing exquisitely*

*Being in the world with ease, grace, elegance and your own personal power*

*Fueling your body with nutrition to look and feel amazing*

It was such a perfect movie and I had the added takeaway bonus of being so happily inspired to enjoy a sexy, luxe and svelte life. If you would like to be inspired and make your husband very happy at the same time, may I suggest you offer up *Spectre* as the evening's viewing?

Now, back to real life and real role models, here

are some of my favourites as it pertains to money and success:

**Warren Buffett**. He did not start to become wealthy until after he was fifty. Despite his late start, he is now one of the richest men in the world. He still lives in the same house, drives a normal car and has the same wife he started out with. Money has not turned his head.

What I take from Warren's example is to live the life you want to and remember your core values.

**Joan and Jackie Collins**. Joan made her own way in the world, ever since she left England for Los Angeles in her early twenties. She became a movie star and her late sister Jackie followed soon after. Jackie became a best-selling and prolific author from observing those around her. These sisters are so inspirational to me because everything they have, they earned themselves, and even though they have a flashy personal style and certainly have lived the Hollywood life, they have remained ladies.

What I take from Joan and Jackie is to live life, have fun, work hard and enjoy making your own money in a way that is true to you.

**Kim Kardashian** (and Kris Jenner). No matter what you think of the Kardashians, there is no doubt that they are an extremely financially successful family. From what I have seen, Kim is an intelligent, hard-working and business-focused young woman. I do not like many of the things her family does, however I can be inspired by the good points Kim and her mother portray. They have taken their strengths (family, glamour, fun) and made it into their brand.

What I take from Kim and Kris is to focus on your strengths, work hard and make hay while the sun shines. I love this quote from Kim: '*You have to stay committed. Some people start and stop, or get a bit lazy. Every year my mom and I write out a goal sheet*'.

**Aerin Lauder** (and Estée Lauder). Aerin is another one whom you would think does not deserve my adoration, since she was born into a wealthy and privileged family. Think about it this way though; Aerin did not have to work as much as she does, because she has plenty of money to live a lovely life as a lady who lunches. She did not have to start her own brand either. I know it is under the family umbrella but still, I am sure it all takes energy and time. From reading about her and her family, they all have a very strong work ethic. And the late Estée built her mega-brand up *from nothing*, seventy years ago, when women in business were rare.

What I take from Aerin is that you can be a successful businesswoman and still be feminine and elegant. You can create your own life in the style you wish.

**Various people I have met along the way**, many of whom I do not know personally. I was serving a retirement-age customer in our store recently and once she had paid for her purchase, she pulled out a tiny well-loved notebook and wrote down the amount she had just spent. 'I *do* like your budgeting system', I told her, I love things like that'. 'Oh I have done it all my life', she said, 'that way I always know exactly where I am'.

Little details like that impress and inspire me so much and sometimes give me new ideas of helpful habits I can use in my own life.

# Chapter 6.

## *Make your own money and be a*
## *success*

When you start looking around at all the opportunities that are out there, it is quite astounding and a wonder that anyone would want to be an employee. I could not see it though; for fourteen years I worked at a desk job and then I left to go into business with my husband. We were self-employed business owners but it was still a job. I had to get up and leave for work at a certain time each day and then stay there all day until we closed.

For a long time, I dreamed of the day when

I could 'retire' from an outside workplace. My desire was to be at home – crafting, writing, reading, housewifing. I did not know quite how that was going to happen, but I put it out there and daydreamed about how wonderful it would be. I would potter around at home all day, hang out washing when it was sunny, sew when I felt like it and cook a nice dinner for my hard-working husband. Yes, I am very traditional at heart.

In 2010, I started my blog howtobechic.com. I wrote for a few years before I burnt out. I felt pressure to post regularly (but it was probably only from myself), I worried if my posts were good enough and I felt a responsibility to my readers. If I did not respond to everyone's comments, I stressed out.

I said to myself (and my husband said it too, because he could see how unhappy I was) *Why not quit your blog, it is not like it is a job, it is just your hobby.* So I stopped, but straight away I missed the writing and connection with my readers. Nutty, I know. After about eighteen months, with my blog traffic still steady and regular emails from readers wondering how I was, I decided to go back.

Little did I know when I started this blog, that I had planted a seed for my future.

## What are your unique gifts that others might pay for?

There are many ways you can earn money – you can apply for a job, get it and go there every day. They pay you to do that. You could get a sales job, sell things and earn commission. Or, you could go into business for yourself, and be an entrepreneur.

When I was an hourly rate employee, I never had the need to think about what my unique gifts and talents were. I thought one of them was organizing and being efficient, but gee, was it boring doing paperwork. Every day I would think, *How much longer do I have to do this for? I have been working since I was 19, is that enough time yet? Can I go home now?*

I would bring books and magazines to read during my lunch break, a bag of lollies for the afternoon; *anything* to make my day a little brighter. The people I worked with were nice enough and it is not like I had a horrible job, but I am a creative at heart and I felt so trapped and bored.

Then when I started writing on my blog and self-publishing after that, I realised *this* was what I was born for. Words! Not only did I adore writing and getting lost in the flow of ideas pouring through my fingers onto the screen, but ladies would write to me personally and thank me for the inspiration and uplift I provided.

That was unexpected to me, because I just wrote about stuff I was interested in, in my own voice. It was especially fascinating because I have always been teased by my family for being too flowery, head-in-the-clouds and not living in the real world.

So to hear from women that I had never met, in countries I had never been to, well, that blew my mind. The more I wrote, the more I realised that here was my unique gift, the reason for my existence:

*I was here to inspire women to live a fun and joyful life without spending a lot of money*

*I was here to encourage women to make little changes every day towards their ideal dream chic life, no matter how stupid other people might think those changes were*

*I was here to share my insecurities and challenges so that women could know they were not the only ones to feel like that*

*I was here to empty out all the ideas in my head*

*so that others could enjoy them too*

*I was here to say 'it is okay to want to live a simple, small and quiet life; it is your life, you get to choose'*

What revelations those were, and now, there is no stopping me. I have so many ideas for books that I cannot type fast enough. I have a list of a dozen to write and still more arriving in my head every week. I suspect the list will grow longer and longer and I will never reach the end of it. What a fantastic problem to have!

What is it for you? What could you do all day and never look at the clock? Can you think of ten ways to make money from it? Can you dare to dream that that could be your job? Instead of your actual job? Do not feel like it is too big a question. It is not. It is actually really small and easy to think about.

Remember what you loved to do as a child. What were your hobbies and interests? Would you like to do any of those things now? Were you always noodling around creating things or perhaps you were organizing the kids in your street to help you rake the leaves in your backyard and create 'streets' to ride your bikes around? There will be clues – breadcrumbs – to help you find the answers.

On your list of ideas, start Googling them and see if there is any of them already being done by someone else. This will help you see what is possible and you can then start out with a tiny, first step. You can explore your options whilst still working in your job, which gives you the security of a pay check while your fledgling idea grows.

You have nothing to lose and massive amounts to gain. There are becoming more and more entrepreneurs and self-employed women in business now, with the opportunities afforded to us by the Internet.

The Internet is still so young too; do not think you have missed the boat when you see people further along than you. It has been 15-20 years that I have been connected to the Internet; that is such a small amount of time when you consider how advanced we have become already. Can you imagine how things will look in another twenty years' time? It boggles the mind.

And the universe is always expanding – *there is enough for everyone.* Opportunity and wealth is like the air around us. You never have to worry about the person next to you breathing in too much air and leaving none for you; no, there is enough for everyone and there always will be.

If you think of all the opportunities to earn money in the same way, you will feel so much more relaxed and this will allow your creativity to unfurl. I cannot wait to hear what you come up with.

## How to make money from your blog

When I first started my blog, I did not have advertisements and I turned down emails wanting me to do sponsored posts (not that there were tons of those, but I did not want any). I would tell them *'it is my hobby, so thanks but no thanks'*.

I am enjoying keeping my blog as my own space, and have also tested the waters of monetizing. Initially, I placed advertisements on my blog through Google AdSense. These do not earn a lot, but I receive a payment every couple of months which is nice to have.

I also belong to Amazon Associates where I earn a small commission (4-6%) of anything I link to Amazon via my blog – usually it will be a book or movie I am talking about.

Both Google AdSense and Amazon Associates earn me very small amounts, but I am happy to leave them as is at this stage.

Then came my big dream. For years I wanted to write a book... decades in fact. About eighteen months ago, I published three eBooks compiled of blog posts, again to test the waters. I was very honest and said that these eBooks were made of blog posts, because the last thing I want to do is mislead people. Many people bought these eBooks and they still do.

Next, I published '*A Chic and Simple Christmas*', my guidebook to surviving, I mean enjoying the holiday season. I had the idea for this book in November, wrote for four weeks and published it in the first week of December. Christmas always stresses me out (I do not think I am alone there), so I wrote this eBook as a sort of toolkit to get me through the season.

This book was very successful and I was thrilled. It was my first original content (not from blog posts) book, although the final chapter is a collection of my favourite Christmas posts, including the most beautiful story of a white cat we rescued and tracked down her owner just before Christmas. Re-reading that blog post still brings tears to my eyes.

Six months later I published my first full-length, entirely original content book '*Thirty Chic Days: Practical inspiration for a beautiful life*'. This book had been in my head for decades, and was almost a year total in the writing. It has my heart and soul in it and I am very proud of it.

As of writing, *'Thirty Chic Days'* has been out almost four months and I am thrilled with the response it has received. Twice as many copies as I had hoped were ordered in the first month of release, and it continues to be my most popular book.

I am still working in the business that my husband and I own, and my blog/book income is a nice part-time job for me. Once we sell our business, I hope to make writing my full-time career instead of having to apply for a job and I can see that this is going to happen, which is thrilling.

If you already have a blog and would like to have a go at writing an eBook, what are you waiting for? No-one is going to give you permission to do something like this, you have to decide for yourself and just do it. It is not hard to navigate the Amazon Kindle Direct Publishing website (kdp.amazon.com) and you can also self-publish in print through Amazon's CreateSpace website (createspace.com).

Having a blog first is great because you have an instant audience through the people who follow you. But even if you do not, you can still have a go. If you love to write as much as I do, it is wonderful just to be writing and have the ability to publish it yourself. It really is instant gratification, and who knows where it might lead for you.

## Just do it

Something I have learned, being a procrastinator and a perfectionist is that *just doing it* is the answer. Do not think an idea to death. Do not discuss your ideas with others forever and a day. Too many of my amazing ideas have never seen the light of day because I have done these two things.

With the first one, I would have a flash of intuition and think, *That would be so great!* Then I would start writing down some of the moving parts, think about it a bit more, get scared, analyses it, and then probably talked myself out of the idea, so nothing got done.

Sometimes I even find myself relieved that I have forgotten about an idea I had, because it was too big and scary. I truly do believe that flashes of inspiration are a gift from God and that they are sent to us. It is up to us whether we do anything with them. When I've followed my gut, amazing things have happened. Imagine how huge our life could be if we took every opportunity we received inspiration on?

For the second one, I have learned a hard truth; when you share a new idea with someone because you are excited about it, you dilute the enthusiasm you have for that idea, and all the energy leaks away. You know how an aeroplane uses much of its fuel just getting off the ground? When you discuss an idea with someone before you have made a decent start on it, you use up all the take-off fuel and then you lose interest in the idea. If you still want to do it, it is hard going to get that idea air-borne.

Knowing these two things, when I had the exhilarating idea to give myself a week to finish this book (it had sat half-written for quite a few months); I did not dilly-dally getting into it, and I did not tell anyone my plan at first. I wanted to give myself the best chance at achieving it.

What do you know? I got so much fire under me and just went for it. I could not wait to write each day and was annoyed at my eyes being tired at night and having to go to bed because I wanted to write all night! I only shared it with my husband when noticed my screen one morning and said '*are you working on something new*?' and then when I was almost finished, I mentioned on my Facebook and

Instagram pages that I was almost finished up on a new book.

The danger time had passed though; I had harnessed the energy and completed a lot of the book already.

If I had not learned from past lessons, I would have started talking about my plan to give myself a really small deadline to complete this project, and the energy would have trickled out so that my exciting thought was left looking like a week-old party balloon.

Add to that others' 'helpful' advice that can bring you down: *are you sure that is a good idea?* and *why rush things?* There is only one thing to do when you get a brainwave, and that is to go for it. Go, go, go, run now, do not look back! I promise that you will be thrilled with the results.

## Act immediately

It is important to take on an idea as soon as you think of it, because the energy is highest at that point. *Strike while the iron is hot* is a very wise saying. It has been said that if you do not act on something straight away, there is a very low chance you will *ever* act on it.

As I mentioned earlier in this chapter, when

I was half-way through writing '*Thirty Chic Days*', I had the idea to write a short 'surviving Christmas in a chic way' eBook. At first I resisted, thinking *No, Fiona, commit to one idea*, but this Christmas book kept knocking at my door. So I put '*Thirty Chic Days;* aside for a month while I got the Christmas book out of me; and I am so glad I did now, because otherwise it would never have been written.

Not only was this project time-critical because I had the idea in November, and you cannot exactly release a Christmas book in June, but the energy for my idea was so strong that it just about wrote itself.

Have you ever tried to write a blog post or a work report when your heart is not in it, but you have a deadline? You will know it is not easy to do, and it does not read that well either. You can sense the energy is quite flat as you read it back to yourself, and your reader will sense that too.

There is the flip-side also – you can raise your energy to act on an idea if you want to. Before I write, I make sure I am feeling good. If I have just been doing some admin work before my writing, I read or listen to something inspirational to lift me up and out of the humdrum admin state of mind.

I am not saying to not do your admin; I love

a neat and orderly workspace and home, and it is very satisfying having things cleaned up and put away. However, the organizing mind space is not that creative so you will want to switch to your creative mind.

If I have not gone for my daily walk, I will do that and when I return, my mind is bursting with good stuff to get out and onto the screen.

May I suggest that the next time you have a thunderbolt idea, whether it is a creative idea, a thought to try a new recipe or even a business inkling you would like to look into; do it straight away and ride that wave of high and inquisitive energy all the way into the shore.

## Moving forward on an idea

A great, but cheesy analogy came to me the other day. I imagined myself getting into the car to go somewhere, maybe to my sister's across town. Because it is a bit of a dog leg with many possible routes, I always wonder if I am taking the best route and what traffic will be like on the route I have chosen.

Do you think it would be helpful for me to putter along slowly, pulling to the curb often, not being confident to put my foot down on the pedal because I am thinking *'Oh, I don't know exactly how to get there, or if I am even going in the right direction. I don't know what's around the corner – are there roadworks? Ooh, is that a sale in that shop?*' and I limp along in my car, one foot on the accelerator and the other on the brake.

That is not what you do at all when you drive somewhere, is it? No, you know that you will figure it out as you go along if you are not 100% sure of the directions. You will see along the way where you are meant to go, because you take note of the signposts.

You put your foot on the gas and drive confidently, because you know if you carry on, you will get there. You already know your desired destination, and even if you go down a wrong street you can just turn around, or go the extra block and then get back on course.

Thinking through this analogy can really help speed up your progress on something you have been dithering on. Just put your foot down already!

### Write your goals down every day

One of my favourite motivators, Brian Tracy, often talks about writing your goals down every day. He says there is magic between the paper and the pen, and that this action activates your brain in a far greater way than simply thinking about your goals, or even typing your goals into a computer. The keyboard is not as mighty as the pen, it seems.

Brian suggests having a small notebook where you take a page to write out your top ten goals every day. It is a very powerful method. When I am writing my goals down, I allow myself to feel how wonderful it is going to be when I achieve them, and I know I will.

It is fun to mix up smaller goals with bigger goals too. Some of my goals are a year or two away, like the kind of home I would like to live in (complete with walk-in wardrobe) or an amount I would like to save; and some are closer, such as a holiday I would like to take. You can do a quick list one day, and you can add a few more details as you dream another day.

Just allow yourself to feel how amazing it will be when you achieve those goals. When I write down that I want my husband and I to go on a one-week holiday to Hawaii before Christmas this year; I can feel the sun on my skin, the excitement of American shopping and the relaxed blissfulness of strolling around together, hand in hand, simply enjoying being together and on holiday. It feels so good!

And that is the key to drawing those goals to you — that feel-good energy; so why don't you find a tiny notebook to keep in your bag and dedicate it to your life's dreams, starting today by writing down your top ten goals.

A quick tip from Brian — he says to write down the day's goals *without* looking back through the notebook. Go entirely on memory and wishes, and then your desired goals will float to the top over time, like cream on milk. The fleeting or unimportant goals will disappear of their own accord.

I like to date each page too, because I imagine myself looking back in two years' time saying to myself, *'Wowee, I have achieved everything on this list!'*

## Be a shining example to influence others

If you don't have a financial mentor to look up to in real life, become one for yourself. Educate yourself around money to show others around you that it is possible. They might not know every last detail of your bank account or investments, but they will sense something different about you.

I've heard it said that the way you do money is the way you do everything. It makes sense, doesn't it? If you are sloppy and slapdash in your financial life, it is likely you are that way with your home organization and other areas of your life too. Therefore, it stands to reason that by cleaning up your money world, you will clean up other parts of your life too. The forward momentum and increased self-worth you'll receive will see to that.

By the same token, I find that when I eat better quality foods and snack less, there is a flow-on effect to other areas of my life. It's the same with money. I feel more in control when I know where my bank accounts are at, what my financial goals are and how much is going in and out of my life, not just with money but with everything.

Be a shining example to yourself and to others. Your success is sorely needed in this world where many people feel downtrodden and like they have no control. They do have control; they just don't know where to look or what to do. Be that beacon who people want to be around, because they know you are learning how to put it all together.

You don't have to be perfect, you just have to start.

# Final tips

No matter how you have been with money in the past, you can change. The past does not represent the future; it does not have that power. What you did in the past was the best of your ability with the knowledge you had at that time. Know that you can change if you want to; it is actually easy to change and sometimes it can be done in an instant when you make a decision.

If someone has told you that you are hopeless with money before, let it go. In your mind, say *'thank you for that'* and then send the message back to the giver. You can be an amazing manager of money. Decide just how amazing you want to be... and be that!

The creative ideas inside are of you worth a lot too, they are priceless in fact. How do you think every other successful fashion designer, writer or app mogul got started? With an idea. And you can too. Anyone can and there is no-one holding us back but ourselves. No-one is going to give you permission to start an idea; you have to give it to yourself. If you need permission, I grant it to you now. Go on and do great things – I know you have it in you.

Do not worry about what your family and friends will think; this is your life, not theirs. Most people are content to live a safe and comfortable life where they go to work and come home, then do it all again the next day until they are 65. Maybe you want something different like I do? The thought of going into an office job filling in the day with paperwork until I was 65 was very depressing. With all the creative ideas flowing out of me, it was just not possible to stay in that environment!

If you feel the same way, I encourage you to dream big and do something about it. There has never been a better time to start your own business and we are so lucky to have the Internet; it really is changing how people live their lives.

And to finish, I would love to share with you

*100 ways to be financially chic.* I wish you all the best with your money journey and hope you have found many nuggets in this book to implement straight away.

## 100 Ways to be Financially Chic

1. Know what is going in and out of your bank accounts

2. Look at doing something on the side of your main job to earn more money

3. Look to others who are doing well financially and see what they do that is different to you

4. Share your dreams with your other half – 'team work makes the dream work'

5. Take full advantage of any workplace savings or superannuation scheme

6. Be inspired by others' successes and know that you can do the same if you want to

7. Know that the sky is the limit and that there is no cap on what you can be, have and do

8. Educate yourself about money, business and finance – choose something to study

today whether it is the business section of the newspaper, a personal finance blog or a library book

9.    List ten ways you can live more luxuriously on your current budget

10.   Find out what your money beliefs are – write them down and ask yourself if they are true

11.   Change your view on looking after your money – think of it as fun and exciting and that it is the gateway to a fabulous life

12.   Know that you have the ability to help causes close to your heart more if you are wealthier – it is not selfish to want to be better off financially

13.   Simplify your life for more abundance – by doing this, you will discover the truism that is *having more with less*

14.   Choose to live well no matter your income – impeccable manners, beautiful posture and cleanliness of the home and body costs nothing

15.   Choose one regular expense to cut out for a month and see if you miss it – perhaps a coffee (make it yourself), newspaper (read

it online) or weekly shopping trip for fun (declutter your closet instead)

16. Browse social media for inspiration only if it motivates you – if it makes you feel 'less than', skip it – read an inspiring website instead

17. List all the ways you are rich already – I bet you can get to 100

18. Make sure that the items you surround yourself with are clean and in good repair – if not, do what is necessary to make them that way or discard them

19. Choose a number of items that you would like your wardrobe to be under and stick to it

20. Get creative with outfits in your closet – have a session where you lay out combos on your bed that you have not yet tried

21. Clean your jewellery so that it sparkles

22. Create new no-spend rituals – brunch at home on the weekend, a picnic in the park in summer, cozy movie afternoons in your living room in the winter

23. Make your home as welcoming as you can – style it as if you have guests paying to

stay *Airbnb*-style and enjoy the results yourself

24. Find money mentors who inspire you and top up on their inspiration often

25. Remember your 'why' – why are you doing what you are doing? Remember the grand vision you have for your life

26. Dream big dreams – even if you do not achieve all of them, you will reach further and therefore get further than you might have otherwise

27. Do not think bad things of people who drive past in an expensive car or flash their cash – know that you could have all those things too if you wanted to (whether you want to is another story)

28. Work out your priorities so that you know what you want to spend your money on

29. Move quickly on a great idea when you have a brain flash – speed is essential

30. Have a goals notebook and write down your top ten goals every day

31. Be a shining example to others by working on your money management skills

32. Speak positively about everything in your life as much as possible, especially your finances

33. Brainstorm ten ways you can make some extra money right now

34. Choose one utility bill to research whether you can get a better price elsewhere

35. Have a no-spend month where you buy *only* the essentials – get creative

36. Focus single-mindedly on your greatest goal of the moment (for me, it is completing this book)

37. Take exquisite care of everything you own

38. Have pockets of luxury for fun – coffee or high tea somewhere fancy, or a night away

39. Surround yourself with beauty – pick flowers at home, stack picture books for effect, arrange the cushions on your sofa, move pictures around

40. Keep your vibration high by doing things that make you feel good – listening to music, moving your body, watching a funny or stylish movie, re-reading a favourite book

41. Become a completer of tasks – finish jobs off properly

42. Increase a debt repayment by 10% - set it and forget it

43. Make purchasing decisions slower – do not rush out and buy something the moment you think of it

44. When you need to replace something, choose quality if possible, but first consider if you need to buy a replacement or can you make do with something else, or nothing at all

45. Think in terms of 'opportunity cost' – look at items you have bought and now do not use; could this money have been put elsewhere for a better 'return'?

46. Make a wish list/gift list of things you would like or need so you have ideas to hand if someone asks you if you have any gift requests

47. When you go to replace a grocery item, try the cheaper option; you can always go back to your original later if you do not like the cheaper option as much

48. Choose one meal that you normally buy or eat out, and make it at home

49. Clean out your pantry and make it your mission to *eat everything* before you buy more groceries!

50. Try not buying groceries for a week except for fresh items if you need them (dairy, meat, vegetables and fruit)

51. Have a freezer stocktake – remove everything, and working quickly, note all items down on a pad of paper – guaranteed you will find more than you thought you had

52. Use up or throw out mystery foods in the freezer

53. Join the library if you are not already a member and you are a frequent book, magazine, CD and DVD purchaser

54. Propose a low-cost Secret Santa this Christmas instead of everyone buying everyone else gifts

55. Ask yourself 'if I won the lottery, how would my life change?'

56. Identify your key values and live your life by them – some of mine are simplicity, peace and creativity

57. If your linen closet is overflowing, take everything out and only put back the newest items, donating everything else to your local women's refuge or animal shelter

58. Feel excited for your abundant future, which starts with what you are doing *today*

59. Make health a part of your wealth and look after it like the precious jewel that it is

60. Delete habits and thoughts that make you feel poor and broke

61. Curate your 'rich girl wardrobe' and design your capsule collection from pieces you already own

62. Commit to being debt-free and do whatever it takes to get there

63. Ask yourself – what do you love to do that people would pay you for

64. Show people – do not tell – how well you handle your finances

65. Make a decision to be a role model to the children in your life when it comes to money

66. Check your bank account every day

67. Choose to be content with what you already have

68. Apply the old mantra (from the 1940s): 'Use it up, wear it out, make it do, or do without'

69. Always pick up any coins you see in the street and say 'thank you' for them

70. Declutter your wallet or purse – tip *everything* out and only put back the essentials; file or trash the rest

71. Consider going on a cash budget where you withdraw a certain amount each week – once it's gone, it's gone until your next payday

72. Start an investment account for your future wealth – see what the minimum investment amount is and go for it; I love tracker/index funds for their lower fees, transparency and simplicity

73. Sell or donate unwanted items; you may raise some cash which is great, but the

most important thing is that those things will be gone from your house

74. Affirm to yourself that you are good with money, and that you are attracting prosperity and abundance to you more and more each day

75. Teach your children about money by including them in age-appropriate discussions such as choosing to not buy something so that that same money can be put into the family vacation fund

76. Instead of focusing on how you can make money, ask how you can create value for others

77. Ask yourself this question and answer honestly: '*Why am I in the financial situation I am in right now and what could I do to make things better?*' – listen for any excuses you might have

78. Get comfortable with being a salesperson – in life we are selling ourselves every day, whether we realise it or not

79. '*Do more than what you are paid for so that you can get paid more for what you do*' – taking this on board is a fast way to increasing your income

80. Put your coins into a jar during the year for a nice bonus at Christmas (this is my father-in-law's tip – he says it's amazing how little bits each day add up to a lot at the end of the year)

81. Automate everything you can – bill payments, savings etc

82. Remove negative words about money from your life – instead of 'I can't afford this', say 'I'm choosing not to buy this right now

83. Inspire yourself by reading autobiographies of successful, self-made people in industries you are interested in (I love cosmetic and fashion autobiographies)

84. Become a money magnet by appreciating all that you have right now

85. Make donations to charities that are close to your heart

86. Surround yourself with people who have a positive mindset

87. Remember the old saying 'neither a lender nor a borrower be'

88. Only lend money to family or friends if you consider it a gift not a loan, then you won't be upset not to receive it back

89. Think in terms of cost per use when making a purchase – the higher price, higher quality item will likely win

90. Move quickly when you have a good idea

91. Change mortgage payments from monthly to fortnightly – not only will you effortlessly pay one extra payment but you will pay less interest overall

92. Have good money boundaries – say no to anything that makes you feel uncomfortable

93. Do not invest in anything you don't understand

94. Make double portions on meals where this is appropriate, for example, spaghetti bolognaise, meatloaf, casserole – put extra portions in the freezer for a quick meal on a busy night

95. Make lunches from leftovers – we have had so many delicious lunches this way – pizza, curry and rice, cottage pie

96. Talk about money with your spouse, especially if you are stressed or hiding something; having things out in the open always feels better - 'a problem shared is a problem halved'

97. Have a savings plan – it is fun to see how much your savings will add up to in a year, five years, ten years; there's interest of top of that too

98. Forgive yourself for money mistakes you have made in the past – we've all had them

99. If you shop to feel better, ask yourself why and be honest – learn to deeply and completely love and accept yourself exactly as you are

100. And finally, be thankful you are the age you are in the time you are living in right now – you are exactly where you are meant to be and it is your time to be prosperous and fabulous, right now – enjoy it!

# About the author

Fiona Ferris is passionate about, and has studied the topic of living well for more than twenty years, in particular that a simple and beautiful life can be achieved without spending a lot of money.

Fiona finds inspiration from all over the place including Paris and France, the countryside, big cities, fancy hotels, music, beautiful scents, magazines, books, all those fabulous blogs out there, people, pets, nature, other countries and cultures; really everywhere she looks.

Fiona lives in beautiful Auckland, New Zealand, with her husband, Paul, and their two rescue cats Jessica and Nina.

To learn more about Fiona, you can connect with her at:

*howtobechic.com*
*fionaferris.com*
*facebook.com/fionaferrisauthor*
*twitter.com/fiona_ferris*
*instagram.com/fionaferrisnz*
*youtube.com/fionaferris*

Fiona's other books,
all available on Amazon:

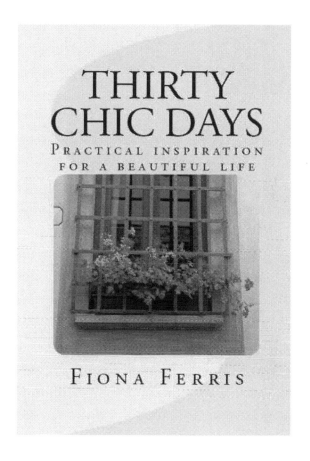

*Thirty Chic Days: Practical inspiration for a beautiful life*

*A Chic and Simple Christmas: Celebrate the holiday season with ease and grace*

*How to Live Well - Chic Inspiration - How to be Slim and Healthy (3-in-1 book)*

*How to Live Well: Simple and practical inspiration to enjoy your everyday life*

*Chic Inspiration: Imaginative ways to live a more magical life*

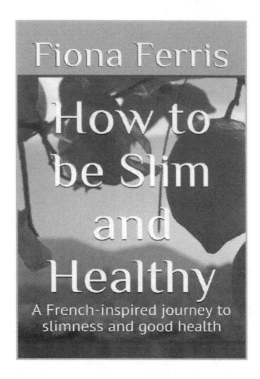

*How to be Slim and Healthy: A French-inspired journey to slimness and good health*

15259160R00102

Printed in Poland
by Amazon Fulfillment
Poland Sp. z o.o., Wrocław